IMAGES OF WAR
B-17 MEMPHIS BELLE

RARE PHOTOGRAPHS FROM WARTIME ARCHIVES

GRAHAM M. SIMONS

WITH DR HARRY FRIEDMAN

Pen & Sword
AVIATION

First printed in Great Britain in 2012 by
PEN & SWORD AVIATION
an imprint of
Pen & Sword Books Ltd,
47 Church Street,
Barnsley,
South Yorkshire.
S70 2AS

A CIP record for this book is available from the British Library.

ISBN 978 1 84884 691 3

Printed and bound in England
By CPI Group (UK) Ltd, Croydon, CR0 4YY

Pen & Sword Books Ltd incorporates the Imprints of Pen & Sword Aviation,
Pen & Sword Family History, Pen & Sword Maritime, Pen & Sword Military,
Pen & Sword Discovery, Wharncliffe Local History, Wharncliffe True Crime,
Wharncliffe Transport, Pen & Sword Select, Pen & Sword Military Classics,
Leo Cooper, The Praetorian Press, Remember When,
Seaforth Publishing and Frontline Publishing

For a complete list of Pen & Sword titles please contact
Pen & Sword Books Limited
47 Church Street, Barnsley, South Yorkshire, S70 2AS, England
E-mail: enquiries@pen-and-sword.co.uk
Website: www.pen-and-sword.co.uk

'...The Memphis Belle - one plane and one crew; in one Squadron, in one Group of one Wing of one Air Force....'

So goes a quotation from the documentary film made by Academy award-winning Hollywood director William Wyler in 1943 and released in 1944 to a public that was both stunned and amazed by the graphic, accurate images of war it contained.

Without doubt Boeing B-17F 41-42285 *Memphis Belle* and her crew generate an image that is an all-American icon - and very rightly so too! Indeed, it has been claimed that the *Memphis Belle* is in the top five of the most famous American aircraft of all time, a statement that we would not disagree with in the slightest! It can easily be placed alongside the original The Wright Brothers' 'Flyer', Lindbergh's Ryan NYP *Spirit of St Louis*, Chuck Yeager's Bell X-1 *Glamorous Glennis* and *Enola Gay*, the Boeing B-29 flown by Paul Tibbetts that dropped the world's first atomic bomb.

The legend was created by a little booklet, produced by the American War Department which states that *'In September, 1942, a new Flying Fortress was delivered at Bangor, Maine, to a crew of ten eager American lads headed by Robert K. Morgan, a lanky 24-year-old AAF pilot from Asheville, N. C.*

Proudly, the boys climbed aboard, flew their ship to Memphis, Tenn., christened her 'Memphis Belle' in honor of Morgan's fiancé, Miss Margaret Polk of Memphis, and then headed across the Atlantic to join the U. S. Eighth Air Force in England.

Morgan had told them it was rough where they were going. There would be no room in the Memphis Belle for fellows who couldn't take it. The boys said they were ready.

They took it. Between November 7 and May 17, they flew the Memphis Belle over Hitler's Europe twenty-five times. Bombardier Vincent B. Evans dropped more than 60 tons of bombs on targets in Germany, France and Belgium. They blasted the Focke-Wulf plant at Bremen, locks at St. Nazaire and Brest, docks and shipbuilding installations at Wilhelmshaven, railway yards at Rouen, submarine pens and power houses at Lorient, and airplane works at Antwerp. They shot down eight enemy fighters, probably got five others, and damaged at least a dozen.

The Memphis Belle flew through all the flak that Hitler could send up to them. She slugged it out with Goering's Messerschmitts and Focke-Wulfs. She was riddled by machine gun and cannon fire. Once she returned to base with most of her tail shot away. German guns destroyed a wing and five engines. Her fuselage was shot to pieces. But the Memphis Belle kept going back.

The longest period she was out of commission at any one time was five days, when transportation difficulties delayed a wing change. When the tail was destroyed the Air Service Command had her ready to go again in two days.

Only one member of the crew received an injury. And that says Staff Sergeant John P. Quinlan, the victim, 'was just a pin scratch on the leg'.

The Memphis Belle crew has been decorated 51 times. Each of the 10 has received the Distinguished Flying Cross, the Air Medal and three Oak Leaf Clusters. The 51st award was Sergeant Quinlan's Purple Heart.

Sadly, the truth does not match the legends, but that does not detract for one moment the bravery of all the men involved.

From late 1942 through to the autumn of 1943 a legend was born – created in combat during the days when 'The Mighty Eighth' Air Force was nothing but a 'piddling little force' the aircraft and crew became known to everyone. The aircraft, the returning crew and the little Scottie dog created a legacy that is now iconic. Without doubt today - almost seventy years after much of what recorded here happened - many of the general public think they know the story of the aircraft and its crew. If you stood at Mud Island, Memphis, Tennessee when the aircraft was on display there, if you go today to see it at the Museum of the United States Air Force just outside Dayton Ohio, or if you talk to the visitors at the Tower Museum Bassingbourn England, it is very clear that they are not only very familiar with the story, they are very comfortable with all that they think they know. One is almost certain that many feel that they are making a pilgrimage, either to see the aircraft, or to visit its spiritual 'home' at USAAF Station 121. However, much of what they think they know is in fact based on what at best can be called propaganda - at worse plain and simple lies.

When all the layers of embellishments, fantasies, rhetoric and propaganda are removed, after all the political machinations and commercialisations are discarded, then perhaps something approaching the true legacy can be seen - and just what an incredibly important one it is as well, for it could be argued - and it is a view that we as authors and historians firmly take - that this single aircraft and her returning crew played a hugely important part in keeping the United States of America in the European conflict, and thus allowed the war there to be won.

Bring all of this together - the combat missions, the War Bond Tour and the William Wyler movie - and this then, is without doubt the direct and lasting legacy of those men and women who built, serviced, supported and who flew 41-24485 into combat. They enabled the aircraft and crew which toured the USA to keep the American public on the side of the Army Air Force during those dark days of 1943 when 'good news' was such a scarcity - and through deliberate timing in the general release of William Wyler's movie, the War Department prepared the American public for the coming invasion of Europe in 1944.

Say these words loud and proud - and let them resound long, loud and clear into the future - those returning ten men and little Scottie dog aboard that single aircraft kept a nation supporting its Eighth Air Force in the European Theatre of Operations. They solely were the spark, the trigger, the catalyst that allowed the build-up to defeat Adolf Hitler and Nazism. Through William Wyler's movie, they also put the American nation in a positive frame of mind for the invasion of Europe.

It is a legacy that each and every descendant of those people can be immensely proud of - for this is the real legacy of the *Memphis Belle*.

The returning crew of the Memphis Belle are seen in a photograph taken some time after their 25th mission.

They are, from left to right: Harold P. Loch - Top Turret gunner; Cecil Scott - Ball Turret gunner;
Robert 'Bob' Hanson - Radio Operator; James 'Jim' Verinis - Co-Pilot; Robert K Morgan - Pilot;
Charles B 'Chuck' Leighton - Navigator; John P 'JP' Quinlan - Tail Gunner; Tony Nastal - Right Waist Gunner;
Vinson 'Vince' Evans - Bombardier; Clarence E 'Bill' Winchell - Left Waist Gunner.

Supposedly taken on completion of the 25th mission, eight of the crew pose with William Wyler as crew chief Joe Giambrone paints on the 25th mission symbol. It can be clearly seen that although there is a swastika under the nose window, the additional eight have not yet been painted under the mission symbols. These, along with the crew names and other 'amendments' were done for publicity purposes to the definitive combat colour scheme.

THE GIRL...
THE NAME...
THE ARTWORK

'Heres a young lady a pip -
She's definitely smart as a whip.
I'll tell you a secret and this is no joke,
This brilliant young lady is Margaret Polk'.

So read an entry in a 1939 scrapbook at Hutchison School, Memphis, along with a quote 'Margaret Polk - Trouble sits but lightly upon her shoulders'. The picture on the right is from the same scrapbook -she would have been seventeen years old.

Margaret met Bob Morgan, the pilot of the *Memphis Belle* at Walla Walla Washington during the 91st Bomb group's training there.

Margaret Polk had been born on December 15 1922, a descendant of America's eleventh President James Knox Polk of Nashville, Tennessee. Her father was a lawyer, a lumberman and a planter in the old southern tradition. 'My daddy was Oscar Boyle Polk. My mother we called her Bessie Rob. She was from Indiana. Her real name was Mary Elizabeth but everyone knew her as Bessie'.

The Polks by now lived at 1095 Poplar, assisted by two black servants, Robert and Alberta Thomas. Margaret was one of four childen but one, Virginia, died not long after birth. Of her three surviving siblings, eldest was Oscar Boyle Jr who was born in 1916, Elizabeth born in 1918 and Thomas Robert born in 1926. Margaret grew up becoming something of a tomboy, despite her attendance at girls' private schools. Brother Tom recalls that as a youngster Margaret had the family nickname of 'Tooker', which remained with her all her life.

'I went to the Miraculous School. It was a little two-room schoolhouse and it had these two old maids. You went up five grades there. It was Miss Emma Cook's School, right there on Jefferson and Bellevue. One old lady had one room the other old lady the other. You could go from that five grades through there, then to the seventh grade at Miss Hutchisons School. We didn't have homework because they said they didn't believe in grading the parents' papers. And it was play, because those old ladies would get out and play with you. They would lift up their skirts and run and play whatever games we used to play.'

There were many pictures taken staged by the press of Margaret Polk, showing Miss Margaret looking longingly at a portrait of her beau.

During the summer she went to the family's farm down at Hickory Valley, Tennessee, some fifty miles to the east of Memphis. There they had a big white wooden house held together by wooden pegs, heated by fireplaces in the winter and with a separate kitchen. On the farm she was more or less allowed to do as she pleased - a great deal of which was to play with the children of the black workers on the farm. Picking strawberries, riding ponies, skinny-dipping in the cow-pond and hoisting the porch furniture into the trees as a prank.

'Daddy also had a farm over in Marianna, Arkansas, with land he was going to clear. So a lot of the time he was gone, most of the time. You know, back then living on a farm you started working from daylight to past dark and you had to be there. I went there quite a lot. I also spent time with my father in Hot Springs. He had given the Plantation House in Tennessee to his sisters.'

Margaret talked about her life after High School. *'I was in a sorority at Miss Hutchisons. I just never cared about boys or anything. I dont think I started dating until my senior year there. My Daddy told me if I stayed home and went to school in Memphis for two years I could go anywhere I wanted to. So I went to Southwestern [now called Rhodes College] for two years. Even here, I had a couple of boys, but we only buddied around. I was talked into a year at the University of Wisconsin by a girlfriend, but it was not as I expected, so I went back to Southwestern for my fourth year. I graduated Class of '43'*

Neither Bob or Margaret had a clear memory of their first meeting: *'I dont really remember when I first met Bob. There was always so many men around there you never did pay attention one from the other'* recalled Margaret. What turned things into 'something special' was an argument. *'I had made a date with another young man for July 31st...'* remembered Margaret *'... we were real popular out there because of all those men and so few women. Then Bob invited me to his birthday party which happened to be on the same day. I wanted to go to Bob's party and break my date, but my sister and Mac [her husband] would not let me. My brother-in-law said it wasn't done. 'You dont late date. You're not in college now. You're in a man's world now'. So he would not let me go. We had a pretty hot argument about it'.*

As so often happens, the argument drew Bob Morgan and Margaret Polk together. He was smitten - and was not averse to using a huge, four-engined bomber to show Margaret that he was still around! The 91st were flying every day now - and Morgan already had a reputation for buzz-jobs, so while Margaret was still asleep, Morgan made sure the entire neighbourhood would have a wake-up call: *'Here Bob would come, around for our five o'clock. He came in so low and it was so loud, you would have thought he was flying right through my window. The whole house shook, it felt like he was coming in through the window! Bob's full of the devil, but he's a damn good pilot. He could really fly that airplane. It was so exciting!'*

Sometime during the time at Bangor 41-24485 gained a name and a painting on either side of its nose of a girl in a swimsuit. But how had the name and artwork come about?

In the days before television, the public got their news from newspapers, and contemporary newspapers of the day reported simply that the pilot had named his aircraft in honour of his fianceé Margaret Polk, his Memphis sweetheart and left it at that. Bob Morgan: *"...I liked Southern belles, and Margaret was a southern belle, so I just called it the Memphis Belle".*

James Verinis, the Belle's co-pilot and Bob Morgan's buddy, remembered it differently: *"...It was in Bangor, Maine, in September 1942, just before we flew overseas. Bob and I went to see a movie. I don't remember its title. I only remember Joan Blondell starred in it. In the movie there was also a Mississippi River gambling boat and I remember that either Miss Blondell or the boat was called the Memphis Belle. We were walking back to our quarters after the show and Bob suddenly said 'Gee, that would be a good name for our plane, the Memphis Belle'.*

That movie was a Republic picture called 'Lady for a Night' and did indeed star Jean Blondell - with a male lead played by none other than John Wayne. Here is a remarkable co-incidence - the name of John Wayne's character?... Jack Morgan, no wonder Bob Morgan paid attention to the movie!

Morgan himself recalled the story differently - once stating that *"...I was a reader of Esquire magazine. I always admired those Petty Girl paintings they ran every month. I wrote to the magazine and told them what I wanted. They sent me a picture and we painted it on the plane"*

Later he was to claim that he called *Esquire,* got Petty's phone number and called the artist direct, telling him that he (Morgan) would like Petty to draw one of his girls to go on the aircraft. According to Morgan, Petty was gracious about it and was thrilled to be a part of things.

Popular legend has it that the girl on either side of the nose of the B-17 represents Margaret. It does not. The story of the artwork and the background to how it eventually appears on the aircraft is as follows. This particular 'Petty Girl' , shown right, appeared as a foldout in the April 1941 issue of Esquire magazine and is thought to have been modelled by either Petty's wife or, more likely, his twenty-two year-old daughter Marjorie and is captioned "I'm the one with the part in the back'.

As for girl being Margaret Polk, clearly this particular Petty Girl was nearly sixteen months old when she first appeared in different coloured swimsuits on either side of the nose of a certain B-17 - so at very best the painting can only be said to 'represent' Miss Margaret! The April 1941 date also clearly repudiates the suggestion' that the creation of the artwork was at Morgan's request. That edition of Esquire appeared nearly sixteen months before Morgan got his hands on the aircraft that was to become the *Memphis Belle!*

Left: The original artwork's artist George Petty.

With the aircraft named, and the nose art in place, it was time for just one final touch. There had to be a way of getting Margaret on board. Eventually she 'flew' everywhere and on every mission the aircraft did, for Bob Morgan managed to place a tiny picture of Margaret in the overhead instrument panel where the compass correction card would normally have been. His Memphis belle would be aboard the *Memphis Belle* as a form of good luck talisman

When the *Memphis Belle* arrived in England after making the long trans-Atlantic crossing, her first home was to be at an rough and ready airfield called Kimbolton near the village of the same name in the county of Huntingdonshire. A few weeks earlier - on September 13th (some records state it was the 12th) the advance party ground echelon from the 91st Bomb Group, who had crossed the Atlantic on board the liner *Queen Mary*, sailing out of New York on September 5th, arrived.

The 91st BG and the *Memphis Belle* were not to stay at Kimbolton for long. The Group consisted of four squadrons – the 322nd, 323rd, 324th and the 401st. The 91st also brought with them a number of ground units including the 441st Sub Depot.

One of the many 'legends' that has grown up around the 91st BG was that in the very early days whist at Kimbolton, West Pointer Colonel Stanley Wray, Commanding Officer of the 91st BG, heard of the empty airfield at nearby Bassingbourn, flew over with a scouting party, took one look at the superior pre-war airfield with its comparatively luxurious centrally-heated buildings and four huge brick hangars and decided there and then to establish squatters rights and move in! Legend has it that even when the squatters were reminded by High Command that they had no right to be there, the 91st just dug in and held on until grudgingly Command made the move official. It is also said that when Stanley Wray's superior finally located the missing Group, Wray claimed a misunderstanding of the original order.

The camouflaged hangars, domestic and technical area of Station 121 Bassingbourn. In front of the hangars parked on the grass between the taxiways are eight B-17s with a further two parked between the hangars. Also visible are a pair of singled engined aircraft and two Airspeed Oxfords parked in between the hangars.
(USAF via Harry Friedman)

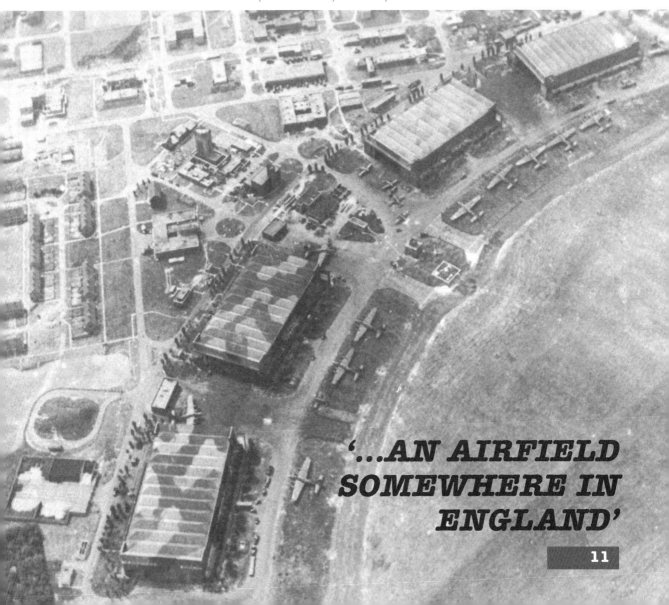

'...AN AIRFIELD SOMEWHERE IN ENGLAND'

However, this was only partly true, for the main reason, as official records show, was that Kimbolton was just too small at that time for a near-combat-ready four-squadron B-17 Group that used around 36 aircraft. It also seems that the runways at Kimbolton were constructed for medium bombers such at the Vickers Wellington and were just not holding up well to sustained usage by fully loaded B-17s.

The 91st diary sheds light on what really happened. Things came to a head during the afternoon of October 11th when Colonel Wray (right) suddenly received an order prohibiting any further flying from Kimbolton, for the recent rains had undermined the foundations of the runways, particularly at the intersections, where large holes were appearing. Urgent investigations revealed that it would take three to five months to rebuild the sections. Clearly, this eliminated any possibility of the Group remaining at Kimbolton. Bassingbourn was more or less vacant.

Bassingbourn had concrete and brick buildings instead of Kimbolton's Nissen Huts - for the 91st BG it was the height of luxury. It did not take long for the Group to settle in to its new home at Bassingbourn. 91st diary October 17th: *'Five intelligence officers sent to various RAF stations for observations and further training. The first Group high-altitude practice mission was scheduled for today. This was carried through successfully and much good experience gained. The last aircraft of the 323rd Squadron arrived this morning. This completes the journey of the air echelon to the European Theater of Operations.*

The Enlisted Men had what was claimed as the largest Red Cross Aero Club in England with a 3,000 book library, lounges, writing rooms, pinball machines and ping-pong. There were two snack bars which served such American luxuries as iced tea, Coca-Cola, grilled cheese sandwiches and donuts. The Officers Club, the former RAF Officers Mess, was surrounded by tennis courts and became a regular country club, hence the stations nickname of 'The Country Club of the ETO'. The Dining Room had a 20 foot ceiling with a skylight. The lounge was a huge carpeted room with long drapes on the windows. The bar had a plentiful supply of Cokes, beer, liquor and wine. Tea was served in the lounge every afternoon!

Due to its comparative luxury Bassingbourn was popular with war correspondents and celebrities alike. Below right: Hollywood heart-throb Clark Gable and Bebe Daniels make a BBC Forces broadcast from Bassingbourn. Gable was over in the UK to make a combat training film. Below left: Hollywood star Jimmy Cagney signs the visitors book in the Officers' Mess at Bassingbourn. *[both USAAF]*

The first mission for the 91st Bomb Group - and the first mission for the *Memphis Belle* - occurred on November 7th 1942. The route was to be from base to a waypoint 10 miles south of Bath in Somerset, keeping below 5,000ft, then climbing to 19,000ft over Falmouth in Cornwall before setting course to target. The route back was maintaining altitude to a point half way across the Channel, then over Falmouth before returning to base. Each aircraft was to carry ten 500lb bombs. There was no fighter escort provided.

Co-pilot James Verinis: *Hardly got to bed when they got us up. We're finally off on our first combat mission. We bomb Brest, in France, a submarine base. Started off with 14 ships but six dropped out half way across because of gun trouble. Made a turn after crossing the coast of France and ran into terrific anti-aircraft fire at our level, 20,000 feet. Three ships hit but none seriously damaged. Ours rocked a couple of times but came through without a scratch. Saw Focke-Wulf 190 go down in flames - shot down by the tail gunner of another ship. Most fighters sat in the distance, not daring to attack. Much damage to target but not completely destroyed. Home to base tired but happy.'*

Almost a month later - on December 6th - it was time for the fourth mission, this time to Lille in France. The target was the Compagnie de Fives Locomotive and steel works complex. It also saw the earliest known photograph of the *Memphis Belle*. The picture shows navigator Chuck Leighton 'patting her ass' for luck at the start of the mission..

Charles B Leighton was born on May 22nd 1919 to Everett and Rudy in Anderson, Indiana. At the age of six, his family along with his sister Ruth and brother Robert moved to East Lansing, Michigan. At Lansing High School the young Leighton made quite a mark in athletics. He set the record of the most touchdowns ever scored there - a record that stood for over 50 years.

He volunteered for enlistment after Pearl Harbor as an Aviation Cadet to train as a pilot. However, after being sent to Maxwell Field in Alabama, he found himself involved in the old Army game of 'waiting'.

'It seems they didn't have enough trainer planes or instructors, so most of us were simply put on 'hold' while waiting to begin flight training. I got tired of the wait, and when we were told that, if we changed to navigator training, we could start at once, I switched'.

41-24639 OR:W *The Careful Virgin* seen parked between the hangars at Bassingbourn. This aircraft was later stripped of essential equipment, packed with 20,000 pounds of high explosive and used as a radio controlled 'bomb' against one of the German V-1 sites in France. The reason for the presence of the visiting C-47 is not known..*[USAF]*

Soon the 91st were preparing for their first Christmas Day overseas, as the Group Diary records...'*All ground school classes were called off on Christmas Day. The only flights that were made during the day were by those individuals who wished to do so on their own initiative. A few combat crews whose planes had received battle damage on the 29th made test flights, but that was about the limit of the military activity on the station.*

At noon a very excellent Christmas dinner was served at all of the messes for both officers and enlisted personnel. At each Officers Club everyone was treated to a drink at the expense of the Commanding Officer.

After dinner in the evening the kitchen details of all of the messes had a party of their own. Many had invited friends to the party and all danced to an improvised orchestra, which was organized after the party had gotten under way. In the evening another spontaneous Christmas celebration took place in the Junior Officers' Club.

During the afternoon approximately 35 of the officers and men accepted a special invitation from the officials at Kings College Chapel. The Services were sung by an excellent boys' choir, and this was followed by a recital of religious organ music. Those who attended the services were more than pleased with what they had heard.

A Christmas party was also arranged for the officer personnel of the American Air Forces by the English Speaking Union in Cambridge. About 20 officers from the Group attended. Tea was served at 1600 hours, and this was followed by informal dancing until 1930 hours.

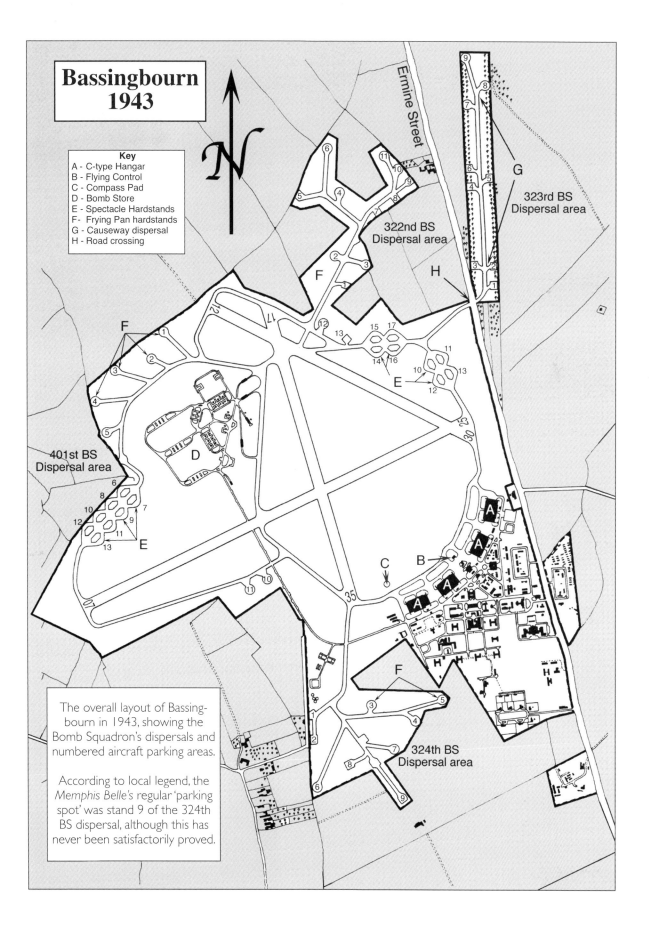

Bassingbourn 1943

Key
A - C-type Hangar
B - Flying Control
C - Compass Pad
D - Bomb Store
E - Spectacle Hardstands
F - Frying Pan hardstands
G - Causeway dispersal
H - Road crossing

N

Ermine Street

322nd BS Dispersal area

323rd BS Dispersal area

H

G

F

E

401st BS Dispersal area

E

D

C

B

A

A

A

A

F

324th BS Dispersal area

The overall layout of Bassingbourn in 1943, showing the Bomb Squadron's dispersals and numbered aircraft parking areas.

According to local legend, the *Memphis Belle's* regular 'parking spot' was stand 9 of the 324th BS dispersal, although this has never been satisfactorily proved.

Four stills from previously unseen footage shot by William Wyler - thought to be preparation for the Lille mission of January 13th 1943.

Top: Bob Morgan signs the Aircraft Acceptance Form while Colonel Stanley Wray looks on.

Colonel Wray adjusts the cords on his life-vest. Bob Morgan, with sidearm in holster has his back to the camera - Just visible, and not in flying gear is Major Aycock, the 324th Bomb Squadron Commander.

Colonel Wray gathers the crew of the *Memphis Belle* around him for one final briefing before boarding the aircraft. The crew were:

Command Pilot -	Robert K Morgan
Co-pilot (presumed) -	Stanley T Wray
Bombardier -	Vince Evans
Navigator -	Charles Leighton
Top Turret/Engineer -	Eugene Adkins
Radio Operator -	Robert Hanson
Waist Gunner -	Clarence Winchell
Waist Gunner -	Harold Loch
Ball Turret -	Cecil Scott
Tail Gunner -	John Quinlan

Colonel Wray in the copilots seat, prior to engine start. Remarkably there appears to be no bomb symbols of any kind on this side of the aircraft nose.

Hollywood Director William Wyler was filming at Bassingbourn from as early as January 1943. Much was done using hand-held 16mm cameras - and to produce the final 43 minute movie he shot over 19 hours of footage, from which this stills have been extracted.

Top: the crew of the *Memphis Belle* arriving by Jeep to the aircraft's hardstand.

Right; Bob Morgan and Vince Evans alongside the nose.

Memphis Belle radio operator Bob Hanson with waist gunner Cas Nastal and Ball Turret gunner Cecil Scott.

Right: on the left is Bill Winchell, on the right is Chuck Leighton with an unidentified officer.

Life on Station - How to get around Bassingbourn!
Right: Four airmen pose on G.I. bicycles that were
used for ground transportation around the airfield
and local area. [USAF via Harry Friedman]

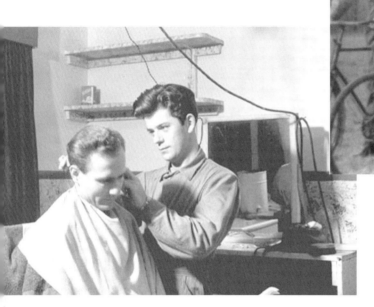

Staying smart - Joe Harlick gets a trim at the Station
Barbers. [Joe Harlick]

Life at Bassingbourn for the crew of the *Memphis Belle* was better than at many of the other temporary airfields that were springing up all over England, as the 91st diarist recorded: *Many of the officers and enlisted men have succeeded in building up valuable contacts with the civilian population in the general vicinity of the airdrome. These constitute an invaluable asset to the morale of the Group. In addition to these connections, most of the officers and men have now become familiar with the better hotels, restaurants, and other places of entertainment and amusement in the neighboring towns of Royston, Baldock, and Cambridge. Many others have become familiar with London and some have spent several of their off days in going to these places to attend theaters, dances, and other forms of amusement, or to see friends and acquaintances which*

Airmen from the 91st BG
march with flags flying through
the nearby town of Royston.
(USAF via Harry Friedman).

they have made since the organization arrived here. The result of these developments has been to create a much healthier attitude in the minds of nearly all of the personnel of the Group. One may judge that the vast majority of officers and men have become oriented to their new environment and have made the adjustments necessary to enable them to continue to do an efficient job.

A few days later a major crisis was averted when a certain item was finally available on sale in the Station Post Exchange - the PX, having been sampled for the first time at the enlisted mens New Years Eve Party. However, as the diarist recorded further efforts was still needed... 'Coca Cola was offered for sale today for the first time. This Coca Cola, concocted in London, is not quite up to those standards to which we have been accustomed. However, it is a universal hope that the English eventually will learn how to manufacture this product to our satisfaction. All those desiring to purchase Coca Cola had to bring their own canteen cups or other containers, as bottles were too scarce to be allowed out of the PX.'

The thorny matter of 'leave' - as opposed to one, two or three day passes surfaced on 17 January 1943: *Authority has just been received giving Colonel Wray the right to grant seven-day leaves to all personnel who have completed three or more months in the European Theater of Operations. However,*

The PX at Bassingbourn. The large posters of the bathing beauties are for Coca-Cola, and on the shelves can been seen packets of Cheese Tid-Bits, Vanilla Wafers and carton after carton of cigarettes and cigars, all strictly rationed to the civilian populace just outside the airfield perimeter!

Colonel Wray decided against this. The 91st Group is very short of combat personnel, and as a result seven-day leaves cannot be given to members of the air echelon. In view of these facts, Colonel Wray stated that he could not justify himself in granting seven-day leaves for ground personnel, inasmuch as similar privileges could not be accorded to the flying personnel.

The 91st managed to maintain a sense of humour, despite adversity. One example was Lt Frank 'Father' Flanagan's blackout messages. All airfields in England had a system of loudspeakers scattered around the buildings and open areas. The usual announcement made every evening was to the effect of 'It is now blackout time and all curtains and blackout screens will be adjusted and remain in place until 0600 tomorrow morning'. However, Father Flanagan would read something like this in a drawl similar to American bandleader and broadcaster Kay Kayser :

Again we greet your listening ears - to sooth your nerves and calm your fears;
All windows please completely cover, and any chinks be sure to smother.
Tonight when Jerry comes a seeking, be sure your screens are not a leaking!

Later, after the 91st returned from the first USAAF raid on Germany itself, Flanagan read:
In fourteen hundred and ninety-two a Dago sailed the ocean blue
in nineteen hundred and forty-three the Yankees came back across the sea.
And Jerry learned from us today, how we do things the American way.
We bombed those blighters from stem to stern - and Boy did we make their fannies burn.
We want no come-backs from Jerry tonight - so for Pete's sake 'cover that bloody light!'

No talk of the early days of the 91st at Bassingbourn would be complete without mention of the Grand Order of the Rigid Digit. Comradeship and morale had always been high on the station despite everything, and the men of the 91st developed a swashbuckling spirit of adventure. The officers, in the shape of Col. Stanley Wray, inaugurated the 'Grand Order of the Rigid Digit'; an award with the motto 'My God Am I Right' made for those who had goofed spectacularly - like raising the undercarriage before leaving the runway! This is certainly a

Colonel Wray with middle finger thought to be 'assuming the position' for the Grand order of the Rigid Digit.

polite way of putting it, for it is based on the old aeronautic term of 'finger trouble' whereby it was suggested that the sufferer was wandering around with finger firmly inserted into an orifice where the sun does not shine! The award took the shape of a silver fist with the centre finger upraised. Members of the Order were also awarded a replica with blue ribbons!

Colonel Wray was an early, if not the inaugural recipient of the Grand Order of the Rigid Digit back when they were at Walla Walla. On August 11th he was aboard a B-17 that crashed on landing at Redmund Air Base Oregon, luckily without serious injury to anyone. Two days later, on August 13th he did it again in a different aircraft! Another recipient was Deputy Group Commanding Officer Lt Col Basken Lawrence, who on March 4 1943 raised his landing gear prior to take-off instead of lowering his flaps!

HEADQUARTERS
ARMY AIR FORCE STATION 121
Office of the Station Commander
APO 634   (G/A/3)

7 April, 1943.

SPECIAL ORDERS)
            :
NUMBER   200)

        1. Due to the exigencies of the Service, in consideration of
the fact that the Sap is beginning to rise, reflecting with candor on
the thought that in the spring a young man's fancy lightly turns to thoughts
of love (or something), and by the authority invested in the undersigned,
LT COL ROBERT P HARE III 0398992, Hq, 91st Bomb Gp (H), is hereby appointed
STATION MATERNITY OFFICER and MID-WIFE, effective this date, in addition to
his other duties.

        By order of the Baron of Bassingbourn:

                                        NATHAN L. ROBERTS,
                                        Major, A. C.,
                                        Grand Executor.

DISTRIBUTION: Special

Despite the Group being on a war footing and operating constantly in a combat zone, there was time to fraternise with the 'natives', as these pictures show!

It seems that things reached such a level that action had to be taken, as the Special Order from the Baron of Bassingbourn demonstrates!

(USAF via Simon Peters)

Two images that although poor quality, provide a clearer view of the damage done by the explosive shells during the January 23rd 1943 mission. The raid had been an attack on the Lorient submarine pens In France. The *Memphis Belle* had been 91st Bomb Group leader, with Lt Col. Lawrence on board. Just visible also is the small hole made by machine-gun fire in the extreme lower tip of the rudder.

Clarence E 'Bill' Winchell was one of the waist gunners aboard the *Memphis Belle* and kept a diary. Bill was born on November 4th 1916 to Marion and Clarence Winchell in Cambridge, Massachusetts. From Bill's diary: *'Ninth mission today for the "Belle" and her crew - third time in a row as lead ship. Crew the same as always but with Lt Col. Lawrence in the copilots seat. The "old Milk Run" again so we expect the usual hot reception. Had pictures made of the crew and ship, also a short broadcast prior to take-off. Taking the land route both ways today to Brest as our secondary target - both hot spots for flak. It seems too that the Luftwaffe have their more experienced pilots stationed down in this part of France. As it has been the last few times, not much doing until we passed over the 'Hun' airdrome just north of Lorient, but after that, wow, the usual hell in large quantities. Just after "Bombs Away" the Belle was hit by 20 mm fire from a German fighter. The fin and rudder in tatters. Quinlan was fortunate, only dazed for a few minutes. First time the fighters have driven in at us right through the flak barrage. Several ships damaged badly - a couple of B-17s went down from the Group behind us. Fighters stayed with us back to Brest. Over the target there was only six of us - all alone. They should call us the 324th Group.*

Followed another Group right over Brest while they bombed it. More flak, of course - no fighters now. Finally out to sea again and then on home. Upon landing, we of the crew were O.K. but the tail of the ship was hanging in shreds'.

Back on the ground, and the *Memphis Belle* was inspected to see what replacement parts were needed. To get the aircraft back in the air it needed a new horizontal stabilizer, new Elevator, new Vertical Fin, new Rudder...

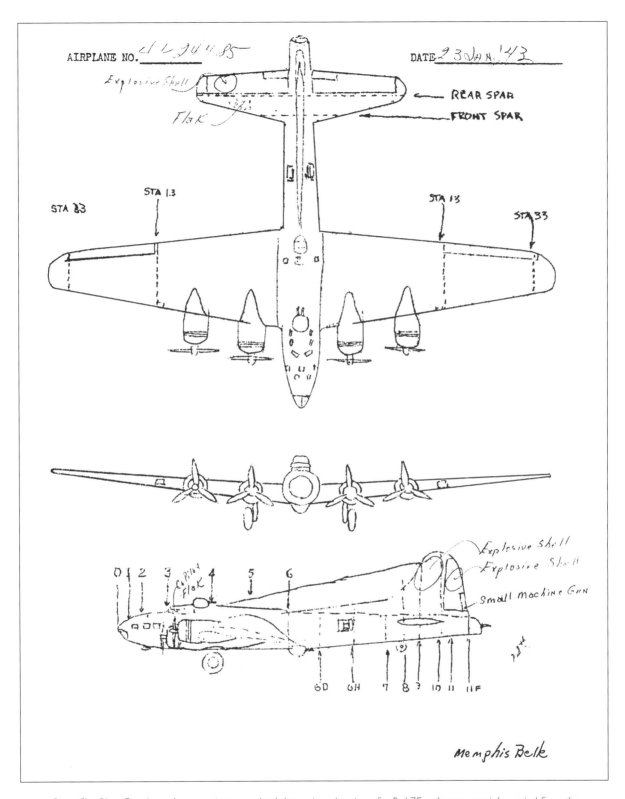

AIRPLANE NO. 4234485   DATE 23 JAN. '43

Explosive Shell

Flak

REAR SPAR

FRONT SPAR

STA 1.3   STA 13

STA 83   STA 33

Explosive Shell
Explosive Shell

Small machine Gun

0 2 3 4 5 6
Co-pilot
Flak

6D 6H 7 8 9 10 11 11F

Memphis Belle

Crew Chief Joe Giambrone's own mimeographed three-view drawing of a B-17F - almost certainly copied from the maintenance manual - showing the location of and the type of damage to ship #485 Memphis Belle on 23rd January 1943. There was damage to the vertical fin, starboard tailplane and elevator and some flak damage around the co-pilot's position.

Quinlan - known by all as 'JP' - was born in Nepera Park, Yonkers, New York on June 13th 1919. After he joined the Air Force PFC Quinlan was promoted to Air Mechanic Second Class on May 16 1942 and then Sergeant on August 1st. Quinlan was assigned to the crew and plane of a young pilot named Robert K. Morgan. JP became his tail gunner.

'Back in the tail, I was the one who got to see most of that. I watched our friends fall back, hit, and the German fighters waiting to pounce on them like a pack of wolves. They always ganged up on a crippled plane. Those guys in the bombers were our friends, and it made you feel bad because you couldn't help them. After that, when they come at you, you want to shoot them. You want to kill them because they killed your friends. You got frustrated because you shot at them and you couldn't stop them from coming in. I was shooting and doing everything right. I was leading them right and firing the guns just right. But they just kept coming. Kept coming'.

Then there was the time when he thought he had been shot through the head. To fire his guns, he had to lean forward and place his face against the sighting piece. He had stopped firing, leaned back and it happened.

'A bullet from an enemy plane went right through my little compartment, in one side and out the other. I felt something wet trickle down my face. When I reached up with my hand, it came away with blood on it. It was crazy but I reached up and touched the other side of my head to see if blood was on that side, too. The bullet didn't hit me. A shattered piece of Plexiglas hit me and brought the blood. I wasn't really hurt. But if I had still been leaning forward in shooting position that bullet would have gone straight through my head'.

On 28 March 1943, the target was Rouen in France and the *Memphis Belle* received more flak damage to the tail area – tail gunner John Quinlan was lucky to escape with a scratched leg.

The view on the left shows a detail view of the flak damage to the tail of the *Memphis Belle*. It is interesting to note that the picture shows a number of things. Firstly, many of the holes show their edges bent outward, indicating that the damage came from the inside. Secondly, there is at least one 'patch', indicating a previous repair. Thirdly, there is a dark area of paint above the word 'Pete' - had a swastika been painted here as a 'kill' that was later disallowed, or was it moved around outboard and above the one visible?

Below: The groundcrewmen apparently marking the damage to the area by flak. Close study shows that the damage has already been repaired, so this must be a posed picture.
[both USAAF via Harry Friedman]

Crew chief for the Memphis Belle was Master Sgt Joseph M 'Joe' Giambrone.

Despite years of searching we have been unable to locate a definitive photograph of the groundcrew that serviced the Memphis Belle. The closest we have been able to come, is the picture on the left, but those in it, although for certain are groundcrew, we have no positive proof as to their identities. Therefore, we reproduce it here with the possibility that they may be those people, but they also symbolise all the other 'unsung joes' that 'kept em flying'! (USAAF via Harry Friedman)

The maintenace crews did much of their work overnight. Unlike many 8th Air Force airfields in the UK, the 91st crews had the luxury of working under cover. Here a B-17F undergoes checks in the 324/401 BS hangar. In the background to the left can be seen one of a pair of A-20s that were on 91st BG strength. [USAAF]

'Flak so thick you could walk on it'. The 91st BG head towards their target while German anti-aircraft fire bursts all around them.

Bob Morgan and Margaret Polk stayed in almost constant touch - this is just one of many letters:

'My dearest Darling

Yesterday was a red letter day for me as I received from you eight letters. I had a wonderful time reading each one over and over again. Then too in one was the announcement of the engagement of the lovely daughter of Mr and Mrs Polk to some lucky 1st Lieut in the Army Air Forces. The announcement was perfect my darling and I feel that your mother deserves a great deal of credit for the job she did. I only hope that early spring dont make things too hard, for I feel that it may have to be a little later than that. You know as I do how unsure things are in my job now. Time will tell and it will be as soon as I return and plans can be made. Nest es pas.

Darling, the peanut candy arrived today and it was sure a wonderful surprise. It only took a month from the time you sent it, so I feel that was darn good time. I have never enjoyed anything so much in all my life as I did that. You are so darn thoughtful about things my love.

I had a wonderful time with my sister and her children. They are so cute and I wish that you could see them as I did. You would feel the same things go up and down your spine. Comprendez-vous.

I got a letter from Dad yesterday and he spoke of hearing from you. He said that the letter was great, but that he had lost it and does not have your address. I sent him that last night. We feel that the best thing you and I can do is to get married and settle down then he will be happy.

That is a good idea of yours to send off more pictures of yourself. I have already sent you some. I only hope they reach you in good condition. I got a nice letter from Mom and as soon as I have the time I shall answer it. You know how little time I have to do anything except work and write to you.

I shall write you a long air mail letter tonight and then I shall be able to write as I like. I send all my love to you my darling, now and forever.
Your Bob

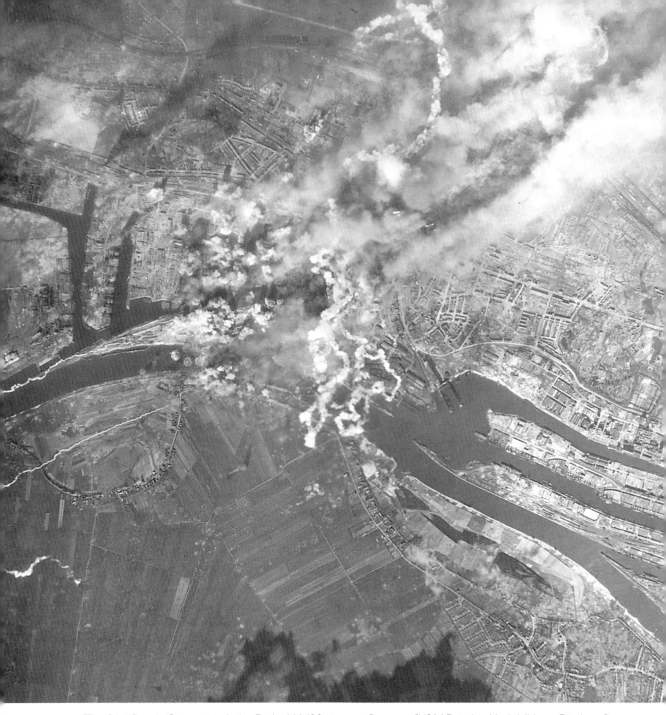

The 91st Bomb Group attack the Focke-Wolf factory at Bremen. *[USAAF via Joe Harlick/Harry Friedman]*

91st Bomb Group mission number 21; *Memphis Belle* mission number 18. The date? April 17th 1943 and they attack the Focke-Wulf factory at Bremen. *This was a mission that everyone wanted to go on. The target was a Focke-Wulf Fw-190 plant and hitting it would be like hitting a tormentor. The 190 has destroyed many of the 91sts aircraft; killed many of their crew. The Memphis Belle would be lead ship of the third Group.*

William Wyler, along with his camerman Bill 'Ace' Clothier had been filming material around Bassingbourn for a number of weeks, concentrating on one aircraft - 42-5070 LL:E named *Invasion II*.

Unfortunately *Invasion II* was one of the aircraft to go down on the April 17th mission. The crew were, L to R standing: S/Sgt C. J Melchiondo, Radio Operator. T/Sgt Goldstein, Top Turret, S/Sgt W W King Waist Gunner, T/Sgt B Borostowski, Ball Turret Gunner, S/Sgt E R Lapp, Waist Gunner. Kneeling, L to R: 1/lt R W Freihofer, Copilot, Captain E M Carmichael, Navigator, Captain Oscar O'Neil, Pilot, Captain E R Bush, Bombardier, S/Sgt A. S. Youell, Tail Gunner. If *Invasion II* had not been shot down when it was, it is likely this machine, not the *Memphis Belle,* would've been the star of the William Wyler movie.

During the winter of 1942/3 Wyler and his crew shot a considerable amount of colour footage at Bassingbourn and at Chelveston. Here 91st BG 41-24480 *The Bad Penny* from the 324th BS has been fitted with cameras in both the waist and radio room hatch positions. Major Wyler (centre) talks to the British war correspondent Cavo Chin. One wonders if Wyler flew this day, for he is the only one not wearing flying boots!

In early May 1943, Sir Stafford Cripps, the British Leader of the House of Commons in Parliament, visited Bassingbourn. He grabbed a photo-opportunity with one of the Memphis Belle's waist guns.

Below: Sir Stafford, General Armstrong and Colonel Wray walk away from the *Memphis Belle*. Bob Morgan is by the wing.

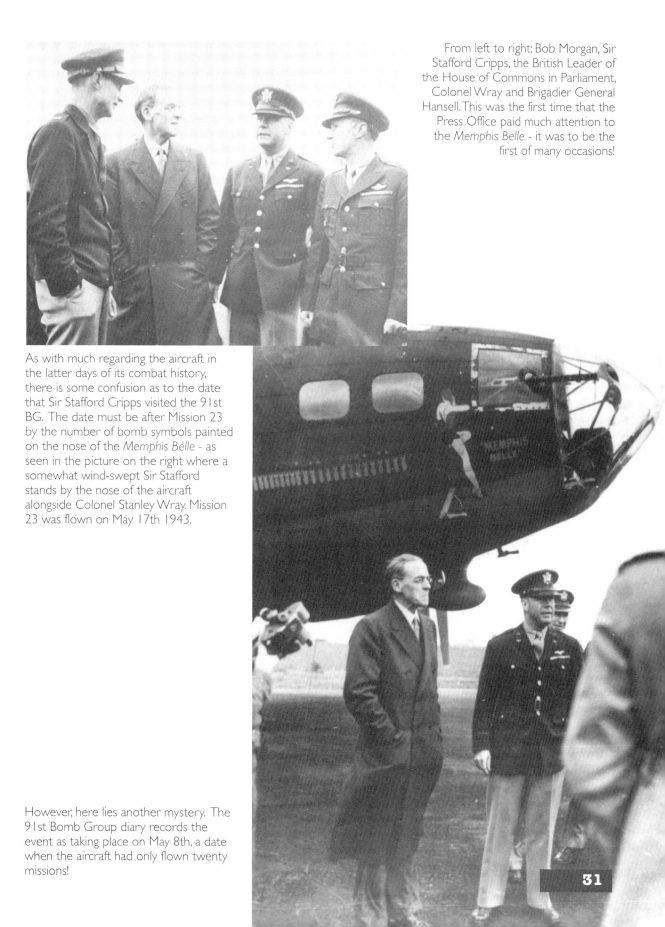

From left to right; Bob Morgan, Sir Stafford Cripps, the British Leader of the House of Commons in Parliament, Colonel Wray and Brigadier General Hansell. This was the first time that the Press Office paid much attention to the *Memphis Belle* - it was to be the first of many occasions!

As with much regarding the aircraft in the latter days of its combat history, there is some confusion as to the date that Sir Stafford Cripps visited the 91st BG. The date must be after Mission 23 by the number of bomb symbols painted on the nose of the *Memphis Belle* - as seen in the picture on the right where a somewhat wind-swept Sir Stafford stands by the nose of the aircraft alongside Colonel Stanley Wray. Mission 23 was flown on May 17th 1943.

However, here lies another mystery. The 91st Bomb Group diary records the event as taking place on May 8th, a date when the aircraft had only flown twenty missions!

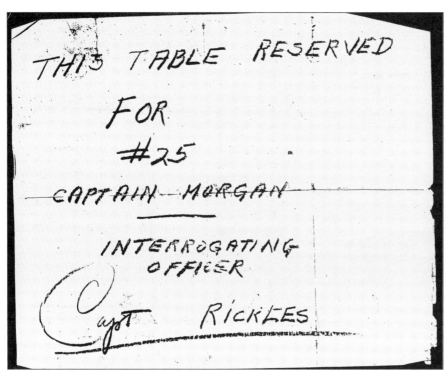

The letter Bob Morgan wrote to Margaret Polk from the cockpit of the *Memphis Belle* as they waited to take off for Morgan's last mission. Morgan's handwiting reflects the stress the crew were under – it translates as:

May 17th 1943

My Dearest Darling,
I am once again writing to you before I taxi the Belle out to takeoff position. You see, this is number 25. The whole tour will be finished. A big load off my shoulders, and yours, too.
There isn't a lot to say but, Margaret, you were riding beside me at all times and, darling, I'll finish this later when I have buzzed the hell out of the field. That is what I have longed to do, my sweetheart. I have both your ribbons on this morning and, darling, may God be with us both.
Well, sweetheart, this is it and so take this kiss and hug and keep me flying, darling angel.
Your Bob

GOING HOME!

Bob Morgan always claimed that this picture was taken on May 17 1943, the day he completed his 25th mission. He said it was taken after the mission for publicity purposes. That may well be the case; however, one thing to notice is that the waist gunner's hatch is closed, not a normal occurance just after a mission. Behind the crew running towards the camera is the groundcrew, headed by Joe Giambrone, recognisable by his flat cap and second from the left. *[USAAF via Harry Friedman]*

One who would not be 'going home' until the war was over was Corporal Tony Starcer. He was the one who painted many of the famous nose arts on 91st BG aircraft and who kept the 'Petty Girl' adorning 41-24485 in tip-top condition. [USAAF via Harry Friedman]

Supposedly taken on completion of the 25th mission, eight of the crew pose with film director William Wyler as crew chief Joe Giambrone paints on the 25th mission symbol. This is one of a series of pictures taken by the base photographic department, using a large format camera that is produced here uncropped, showing the Photo-Lab filing information normally removed by printing.

The whole period between finishing the last mission and 'going home' was a whirlwind of events, ceremonies and presentations. Behind the scenes the transfer had to be arranged moving the men and the aircraft from the 91st Bomb Group records to the War Department's Publicity organisation - something that had never really been done before.

Then there was making all the arrangements to work with William Wyler and his crew. The men and machine may have finished with combat fighting for the moment, but there was others to face - the Press Corps of the UK and America!

Not long after the last mission was completed King George VI and Queen Elizabeth were schedueld to visit Bassingbourn and inspect a number of aircraft. This had been planned for some time, but such was the importance of the return to the USA, it was hastily re-arranged to make the *Memphis Belle* and crew the highlight of the visit!

Right: King George VI and Queen Elizabeth inspect the Guard of Honor at Bassingbourn on May 26th 1943.

The 91st BG record this date as May 15th. Captain Theodore Parker, the Group historian recorded that: *'The King and Queen of England, accompanied by a rather large retinue of officials, gentlemen-of-honor and ladies-in-waiting, visited Bassingbourn just before lunch today. Rumors of their impending visit had been going the rounds for the past two weeks.*

Left: The King is escorted into the Headquarters building.

Parker continues recording the event: *'They arrived in six large, comfortable-looking limousines, at approximately 1115 hours, were met at the gate by Colonel Wray and his staff, received the salute from the guard of honor, and proceeded to give Bassingbourn one of the most cursory goings-over that this old and well-established airdrome has ever had. Generals Eaker, Longfellow, Hansell, and several unidentified United States Army Air Forces officers were also present'.*

Right: the King and Queen outside the Headquarters Building at Bassingbourn on 26th May 1943. A USAAF cameraman winds up a 16mm movie camera to the right of the picture.

The Photo-Lab picture code shows the incorrect date of 15th May 1943.

(GPR-55-12-91)(15-5-43)   QUEEN

Theodore Parker's Log: 'The King and Queen drove around the taxi strip, through the hangars and into one of the dispersal areas. The King and Queen met Captain Morgan and the crew of the rapidly becoming famous 'Memphis Belle'. Captain Morgan did a very good job of meeting the King and Queen and showing them his aircraft. At the conclusion of this ceremony, they returned to the main administration building, where the formal farewells were said. Their visit to Bassingbourn probably lasted all of 45 minutes.'

The stills on this page come from William Wylers 16mm colour footage of the King and Queen's arrival and inspection of the Memphis Belle at their hardstand.

Brigadier-General Armstrong talks with King George VI as he inspects the *Memphis Belle's* groundcrew. Robert Morgan and Colonel Stanley Wray looks on. Armstrong had only taken control of the 101st Provisional Heavy Bombardment Wing at Bassingbourn on May 18th and, as such, was the highest ranking officer on the base and was thus the King's escort.

Below: the Royal party inspects the Memphis Belle's aircrew. The groundcrew were lined up on the other side of the nose. Joe Harlick's photograph below clearly shows a number of interesting details. At this point in time the swastika 'kill' markings had not been painted under the bomb mission markings, nor had the crew names been painted under the windows.

It's clear from the smiles on their faces, in the smaller picture, the Americans were very happy to show the King and Queen of England around the base and it's aircraft. Not only was the *Memphis Belle* displayed - *Mizpah, Delta Rebel No.2* and an unknown B-40 were also on display along with visiting aircraft such as veteran B-24 *Liberty Lass* from the 44th BG at Shipdam in Norfolk.

Previously unseen is this picture showing King George chatting to *Memphis Belle* tail gunner John Quinlan. The feather in the Queen's hat is visible above the shoulder of the crew member on the left, standing adjacent to Ira Eaker who is facing the camera. The visit was reported in at least one British newspaper - with a May 27th dateline - who reported that '...*ground crew chief M/Sgt Joseph M Giabrone of Norristown PA admitted that he felt 'sort of speechless' while talking with the Queen'*.

More views of the royal visit that clearly demonstrate that it was more than just a visit to see the *Memphis Belle*, as later claimed by William Wyler. Above: The royal party chat, while others appear to be watching some aerial activity off camera to the right. The aircraft behind the royal party is an Airspeed Horsa glider. In the distance on the right is almost certainly the *Memphis Belle*.

Below: Queen Elizabeth walks past military transports - the ubiquitous JEEP.

Below: the angle of the heads suggest that there may well have been some form of air display taking place. Colonel Wray is explaining something to the King off to the left, while the Queen watches with two USAAF officers and a British Army Brigadier. Interestingly, the aircraft behind is an Armstrong Whitworth Whitley marked '18' and may well have been used in conjunction with the Airspeed Horsa glider seen in other pictures.

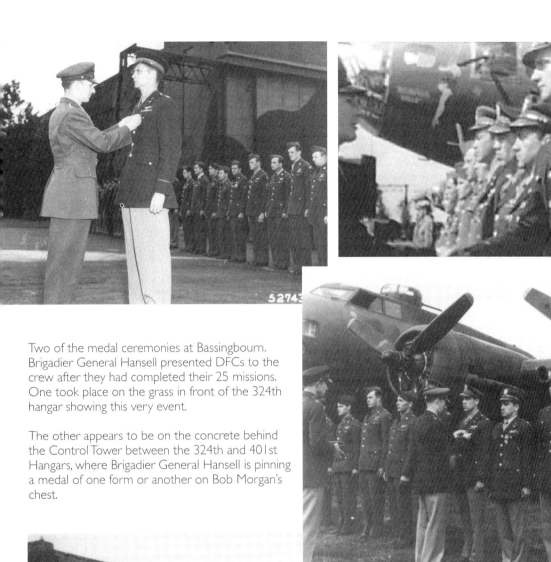

Two of the medal ceremonies at Bassingbourn. Brigadier General Hansell presented DFCs to the crew after they had completed their 25 missions. One took place on the grass in front of the 324th hangar showing this very event.

The other appears to be on the concrete behind the Control Tower between the 324th and 401st Hangars, where Brigadier General Hansell is pinning a medal of one form or another on Bob Morgan's chest.

COPY.

HEADQUARTERS EIGHTH AIR FORCE
Office of the Commanding General

APO 633, U.S. Army
8 June 1943.

SUBJECT: Field Report.

TO   :   Lt. Col. Beirne Lay, Jr., Photographic Section.

Saturday, 15 May, Captain Clothier and the undersigned with equipment and several enlisted men left London for Bassingbourne for the purpose of photographing both ground and air activities in colour for use in the 16 mm. documentary short subject. Stood by to photograph return from mission to Emden and possible battle damage, but return of 92nd Group uneventful.

Sunday, 16 May, proposed mission scrubbed so went on practice flight with Lt. Beasley to Alconbury, made take-off and landing from ball turret and other aerial photography. Conferred with Lt. Elliott at Alconbury on the use of 16 mm. camera by co-pilots. Lt. Elliott has no 16 mm. motion picture cameras for distribution to co-pilots and it is suggested he be supplied with same.

Monday, 17 May, the undersigned with Captain Clothier and Sgt. Slate accompanied mission to Lorient and photographed target and moderate flak from nose of B-17. Uneventful trip.

Tuesday, 18 May, arranged with Colonel Wray to get Captain Morgan and crew of "Memphis Belle" assigned to us for several days when not interfering with operations. Photographed this crew and ship engaged in ground activities.

Wednesday, 19 May, accompanied mission to Kiel and obtained some good shots. This sortie was made with Captain Gaitley in B-17 "Our Gang". Spoke to Mr. Lovett, Under Secretary of War for Air, about contemplated feature picture. He seemed to be interested.

Thursday, 20 May, photography of Captain Morgan and crew and ground activities around "Memphis Belle".

Friday, 21st May, returned to London. Remained in London 22, 23, and 24 May.

Tuesday, 25th May, returned to Bassingbourne at 0100 hours. Arranged with Colonel Wray for King and Queen who were visiting field to inspect "Memphis Belle" and crew, which was photographed in 16 mm. Kodachrome and will make effective finish for documentary short. Spoke to Brigadier General Anderson, CG., 4th Wing, of the activities of the photographic section. General Anderson showed great interest and gave assurance of all possible co-operation from his command.

SECRET

Thursday, 27 May, accompanied training flight with Colonel Gross and got shots of formations. Received information of bomb accident at Alconbury. Tried to Photograph it from the air but it was already too dark.

On Friday, 28 May, returned to Alconbury, and photographed damage of bomb accident. Returned to London at 1845 hours to deliver film and also view developed film. Returned to Bassingbourne same night.

Saturday, 29th May, Captain Clothier and the undersigned accompanied mission to St. Nazaire and some good photography of target, formations and a B-17 shot down by enemy action was obtained by Captain Clothier and Lt. Beasley.

From Sunday, 30th May, to Friday, 4th June, much time was lost due to bad weather conditions. When weather permitted photographed some ground activities, Decoration Ceremony with General Hansell giving D.F.C's to Captain Morgan and crew of "Memphis Belle", etc. At General Eaker's request exposed some film on Sir Archibald Sinclair who was visiting the station on Friday, 4 June. During this period of time these officers were particularly cooperative:

    General Hansell
    Colonel Wray
    Lt. Col Lawrence
    Lt. Col. Reed - Alconbury

A good deal of valuable film for the documentary short subject was obtained during the period of this report. Due to operations and bad weather not everything planned was obtained and a number of shots that are most desirable for the documentary will be listed separately and can easily be obtained by Captain Clothier in the rear future. It is also highly desirable that some additional film of target strikes and fighter attacks be exposed in colour for effective use in this picture, which with a competent commentary, musical score, and sound effects, and a professional job of editing, it is felt will make for an entertaining as well as instructive film of value to the Army Air Forces.

                                        WILLIAM WYLER,
                                        Major, AC,
                                        Photographic Section.

A two page document from one of William Wyler's Field Reports to his boss Lt Col Beirne Lay Jnr. This document corrects many of the myths and legends that have grown up regarding the *Memphis Belle* and crew during this time.

After the war, Lay returned to Hollywood, where he was working in 1946 when he was approached by Sy Bartlett, another veteran of the Eighth Air Force, to collaborate on the novel-screenplay project which became Twelve O'Clock High, published in 1948 and released in 1949, respectively. Lay continued as a colonel in the Air Force Reserve and with fellow reservist James Stewart approached Paramount with a concept for the film *Strategic Air Command*.

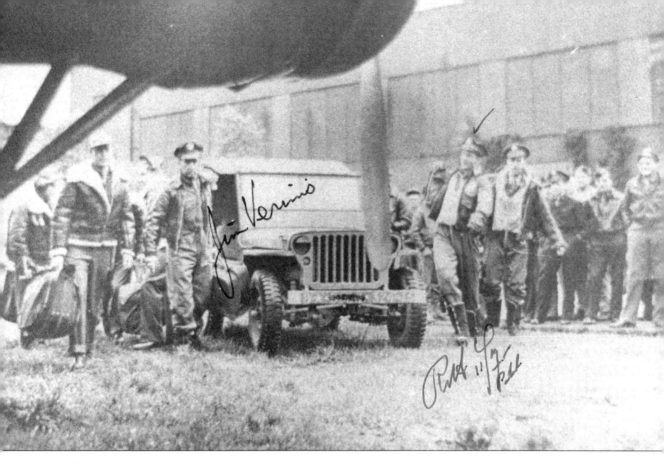

Bob Morgan, Jim Verinis and the rest of the crew of the *Memphis Belle* arrive by Jeep at the aircraft - parked in front of number 3 hangar Bassingbourn - for the start of the long journey back to the USA. This particular copy-print has been signed by Jim Verinis and Robert Morgan.

Right: Jim Verinis, Chuck Leighton and Bob Morgan say 'thank you and good-bye' to the *Memphis Belle's* ground crew. Joe Gi-ambrone, the crew chief is closest to the camera on the right. *(USAF via Harry Friedman)*

Left: Vince Evans, Chuck Leighton and Bob Hanson about to board the Memphis Belle for the journey back to the USA. At least, that is what the publicity said when this picture was taken on June 7th 1943.

Below: Bob Morgan and some of the crew say goodbye to fellow officers at Bassingbourn. Not long after this picture was taken, Morgan was jumped upon by everyone, stripped to his underwear and unceremoniously bundled aboard the Memphis Belle through the waist hatch.

The two famous 'Going Home' pictures of the Memphis Belle as it flies low over the Cambridgeshire countryside By this time control of the aircraft and crew had passed from the 91st Bomb Group directly to the War Department. The new vertical fin and replacement rudder is clearly visible as is the new rear entry door, already sprouting signatures all around it...

The departure from Bassingbourn did not initially go that far - just to RAF Bovingdon, the closest USAAF airfield for Command Headquarters at High Wycombe, for another presentation ceremony.

At Bovingdon Morgan and the crew were presented to both Lieutenant General Jacob L Devers, the recently appointed overall Commander of US Army Forces in Europe and General Ira Eaker. The ceremony was filmed by William Wyler, *Movietone News* and a sound recording was made by the British Broadcasting Corporation. Firstly General Eaker made the introductions:

'General Devers I am proud to present to you Sir the Captain, combat and ground crew of the Memphis Belle, a Flying Fortress which has fought twenty-five successful battles against the enemy. A crew that is typical of the veterans of the Eighth Air Force, who have shown the power of our daylight offensive to our enemy. Captain Morgan and his combat crew are leaving shortly for the United States. This combat crew was chosen for an important home-based assignment because their exploits typify the experience of their comrades. Because the geography of the nation is represented in the eight States from which they hail. Because they have meshed their individual skills into a highly specialised fighting unit - a true combat team. They have met and outfought the best the enemy could offer.

General Devers then addressed the crew directly; *'You are being sent on another mission - perhaps the most important of the many on which you have flown in this famous plane. Yes the most important. But it is not to carry bombs. It is to carry a message which should hearten a great people. This message is to the one hundred and thirty million people of America. I want you to tell them, that all of us over here realise that into this plane has gone all work, the thought and determined courage of countless Americans. They mined the material from the earth, spun the fabric, labored in the forests, mills, factories and offices to create it. Americans built it. I want you to let America know that each man's work and each woman's work is an essential part in the winning of this war. Tell America to send us crews with the knowledge, the training, the determination and courage which I have found with no exception in the*

Eighth Air Force. Pilots like Captain Morgan, copilots like Captain Verinis. Navigators like Captain Leighton. Men who go to and destroy the enemy no matter what the weather or the time of day. Bombardiers who can hit the target with their bombs like Captain Evans. Engineers of the calibre of Technical Sergeant Loch. Radio Operators who perform their important functions with the technical skill of Technical Sergeant Hanson. We want gunners like Sergeants Scott, Nastal, Winchell and Quinlan. These men have damaged or destroyed twenty-five enemy planes. Your ground crew. Sergeants Giambrone, Walters, Armstrong, Champion, Blouser and Corporal Sowers. Tell them of the hours they work to keep you flying. Finally I take this opportunity to commend each of you publicly and to wish you and the Memphis Belle God Speed.

Above: Lieutenant General Devers, Commander ETOUSA, shakes hands with Bob Morgan at Bovingdon before they returned to the USA., watched on by the crew and Major General Eaker.

Right: Generals Devers and Eaker by the nose of the aircraft. (USAAF via Harry Friedman)

BACK IN THE USA!

The location of all the official welcoming ceremonies for Bob Morgan, the crew and the aircraft was Washington National Airport in the nation's capital. It was also the starting point for an amazing nationwide war bond tour. The date? June 16th 1943. Legend has it that when they arrived over the airport, Morgan received a radio message from the Control Tower: *'This is from General Arnold. He has instructed me to order you to buzz the field'*. Morgan did buzz the field - and every other field they arrived at during the tour!

At some stage - most likely in preparation for the bond tour before leaving the UK, for the 'list' is visible on photographs of the aircraft when it arrived at Washington DC - all twenty-five missions were painted in the *Memphis Belle's* vertical fin, along with the names and State of five of the ground crew. Immediately under the serial number - and barely visible on the original print - is Joe Giambrone, then R G Walters, Sgt Lipscomb, C P Blauser and possibly someone called L A Sowers.

This theory is all the more plausible as Joe Harlick who took the original picture was at Bassingbourn before the *Memphis Belle* departed for the USA.

General Arnold and Under-Secretary of War Robert Patterson under the nose of the *Memphis Belle* at Washington National Airport, along with the crew and Stuka, the Scotty dog mascot.

Washington DC to Memphis TN - June 19th 1943. Flight Time logged: four hours.

The aircraft was scheduled to arrive at Memphis Municipal Airport soon after 1pm - and thousands were waiting!

'The Memphis Belle was coming home. And standing on the taxi apron of the Memphis Airport, waiting, was a slim, glow-eyed girl, dressed in a bright summer frock, her heart pounding in anticipation. She was waiting for the man who had held her in his arms, whispered sweet words of love and had asked her to marry him. He had promised to come home from the wars.

Now he was coming, the pilot of the Memphis Belle'

The aircraft and crew were met then escorted by a B-26 Marauder bomber and a P-38 Lightning fighter. , then Morgan buzzed the airport.

The aircraft, the pilot and his girl on arrival at Memphis TN.

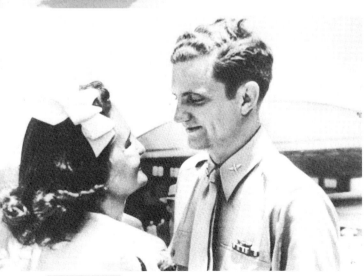

Margaret Polk and the crew in front of the aircraft at Memphis Airport. There were to be many many more photographs of the crew like this taken during the tour.

The Army and the dignitaries had to wait while Bob Morgan hugged and kissed Margaret Polk for himself for her and for the cameras, then, with his arm around her waist, he led his crew into a hangar where Mayor Walter Chandler and other dignitaries were waiting to welcome them to the city. Then there was open-top car parades, there were interviews. Hostesses vied for the attention of the real Memphis belle and her beau to attend their parties. The crew made a trip to the Fisher Body Plant to meet and offer encouragement to the workers of their Memphis Aircraft Division who making aircraft parts and major assemblies for B-25s and the forthcoming 'super-bomber', the B-29.

Bob Morgan made a quick trip to 1095 Poplar Avenue to meet his future Mother-in-law and two future brothers-in-law. They made plans to marry in Memphis, with suggestions that it might be 'sometime in August' but their plans were put on hold. Not by second thoughts, not objections from their parents, but by the military in the shape of the Public Relations machine of the War Department.

It seems that there had been 'discussions' about the young couple's romance and it had been decided that their romance could serve the national interest best by being stretched out until the tour was over. It would add human interest to every stop the Public Relations folks from the War Department thought, if the *Memphis Belle* pilot and his sweetheart were 'about to be married', not 'actually' wed!

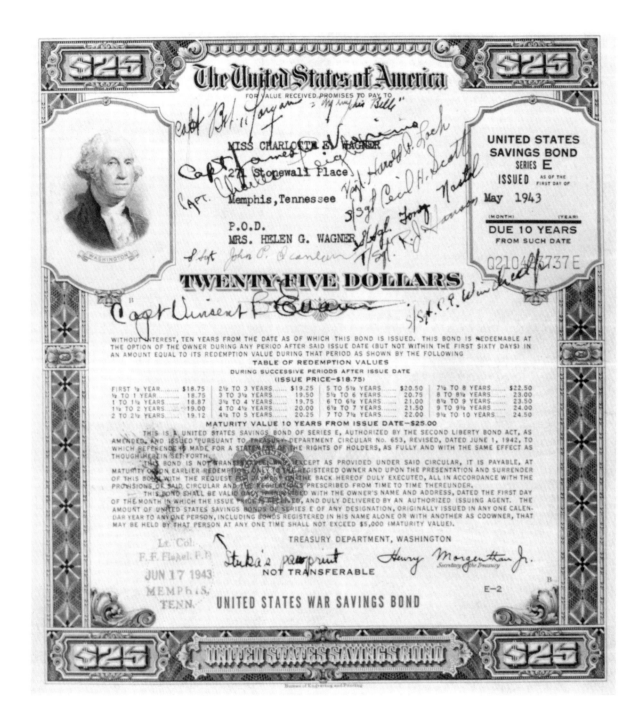

One of the real reasons for the War Bond Tour - to sell these! This particular example - issued to Miss Charlotte E Wagner of Memphis on June 17th 1943 - has been signed by all of the aircraft crew, including Stuka! *[via Harry Friedman]*

It was in Memphis that the real start of all the public and press attention happened.

Right: Margaret Polk is interviewed by radio station WMC, as Bob Morgan watches on from the right.

The Press followed the crew everywhere - interest had started to be created during the last few missions in England when regular reports were fed back to the USA. By the time they made it back there was a ready market for the love-story of the clean-cut pilot and his southern belle fianceé.

It was to be the start of a crazy six weeks or so - Bob and Margaret were photographed whereever they went - even outside her home at 1095 Poplar Avenue, Memphis.

The crew were to be guests at many parties throughout the tour. Here Bob Morgan and and Margaret, along with Vince Evans and his Escort are seen at a party in their honour. *[via Harry Friedman]*

After Memphis it was on to Hartford CT, via Nashville TN. Lining up for the cameras at Hamilton Propellers. Left to Right: Nastal, Loch, Morgan, Evans, Leighton, Verinis, Hanson, Winchell, Quinlan. It seems that Cecil Scott was off talking with a friend in the crowd when the picture was taken!

Right: The aircraft sits in a roped-off area at Hartford. Pitot head covers are in place and somone had taken care to 'dress the props', putting them all in the same place!

Above: another view of the aircraft and crew at Hartford. At every stop there seemed to be a flag-draped platform for speeches from both the crew and local dignitaries.

Left: : Taken at Hartford was this close up of Cecil Scott's 'office' the ball turret of the *Memphis Belle* [both via Harry Friedman]

Memphis TN to Nashville TN - June 22nd
Flight time: one hour fifteen minutes.

Nashville TN to Bridgeport CT - June 24th
Flight time : five hours thirty minutes.

Bridgeport CT to Hartford CT - June 26th
Flight time : one hour.

Hartford CT to Boston MA - June 28th
Flight time: logged: one hour thirty minutes.

The New England Aviation Cadet Committee
requests the pleasure of your company
at Dinner to meet
The Officers and Crew of the Flying Fortress
"Memphis Belle"
on Monday, June twenty-eighth
at seven-thirty o'clock
The Harvard Club of Boston

Cocktails at Seven   R.S.V.P.
Dress Informal   30 Kilby Street, Boston

OFFICE OF THE MAYOR

CITY OF BOSTON   MASSACHUSETTS

MAURICE J. TOBIN
MAYOR

By the time the aircraft and crew reached Boston MA, the invitations were rolling in thick and fast Here are just three of the invitations that were awaiting the crew when they arrived at Boston. They show the scope and scale in the manner of which the crew were féted. They arrived at General Edward Logan Airport outside Boston MA, escorted by a fleet of Republic P-47 Thunderbolt fighters, to be met by Mass. Gov. Saltonshall, Mayor Tobin and other military officials. Throughout the day there was a huge exhibition out at the airport, organised by the New England Aviation Cadet Committee as part of their recruitment drive.
(Robert Hanson/John Quinlan)

His Honor the Mayor

requests the pleasure of your company

at a breakfast to

The Crew of the Flying Fortress

"Memphis Belle"

at the Parker House

at Eight A. M.

Tuesday, June Twenty-ninth

Nineteen hundred forty-three

Please reply to
Lawrence McCabe
Mayor's Office, City Hall
Boston, Mass.

NEW ENGLAND AVIATION CADET COMMITTEE

PLEASE   30 Kilby Street
REPLY TO   Boston, Massachusetts
                  LAFayette 4883   June 26, 1943

Staff Sergeant John P. Quinlan
c/o Memphis Belle
East Boston Airport
East Boston, Massachusetts

Dear Sergeant Quinlan:

         The honor of your presence is requested
at a Luncheon to be given by the Aeronautical
Association of Boston, in the State Suite of the
Copley Plaza Hotel, Boston, on Tuesday June 29th
at 12:30 P.M. Transportation will be arranged for
you from the East Boston Airport.

         The Governors of the six New England
States, representative members of the Army and Navy,
and many civilians actively engaged in the develop-
ment of Aviation will be present. We feel it will
be of particular interest to you, in learning what
is happening at home in this fast growing field of
endeavor.

         The Aeronautical Association has asked us
to extend this invitation to you and we hope that
you will be able to accept.

                      Very truly yours,

                      G. T. King

                NEW ENGLAND AVIATION CADET COMMITTEE

Top: Bob Morgan brings the *Memphis Belle* into the parking area outside the NACA facility at Cleveland. Above: The *Memphis Belle* parked outside the NACA hangar at Cleveland. Right: a 'cutesy' picture that nevertheless clears up yet another mystery is this one taken in Cleveland - yes, Stuka DID have her name painted in the crew entry door hatch! Below: sheltering from the sudden squall but determined to have their picture taken with the *Memphis Belle* crew is left, Edward Raymond Sharp, the Manager of the NACA Aircraft Engine Research Lab at Cleveland from 1942 until 1947 and George Lewis, the Director of Aeronautical Research for the National Advisory Committee for Aeronautics (NACA) from 1924-1947. [all AERL/NACA via Harry Friedman]

It's Memphis Belle In Person: Fiancee Greets Hero Pilot

MARGARET FOLK, ALIAS "MEMPHIS BELLE."

BY MARJORIE WESTERN

A bewildered girl with stars in her eyes and a lump in her throat today walked into her surprised fiance's arms and into

The visit to Cleveland was to be a series of surprises for Bob Morgan - the first being the arrival of his brother and father from Asheville. The reunion took place at the Hotel Cleveland where the crew was having dinner before making a 7.30pm radio broadcast on WTAM. Next day the crew visited Jack & Heinz Inc in Bedford and Thompson Products in Cleveland and Euclid before going to the Addressograph-Multigraph Corp - and another surprise.

Surprise Surprise! Margaret drops in on the War Bond Tour in Cleveland This, and the two other pictures over the page was taken outside the Addressograph-Multigraph Headquarters office complex.
[via Harry Friedman]

Margaret and her mother were secretly flown up to Cleveland by the Addressograph-Multigraph Corporation as a surprise for Bob Morgan. Here Bob greets Margaret's mother Mary Polk with a kiss on the cheek. Margaret is on the right of the picture, with her back to the camera.

Bob Morgan introduces Stuka to the workers of the Addressograph-Multigraph Corporation.

The message put out by the crew at every stop - was 'please support the Air Force in it's efforts!'

Left: Jim Verinis with Stuka getting an official A-M dog-tag from Tom Haslett.

Right: John Quinlan gets a new tag from Jean Bergner, who sets it on a Graphotype.

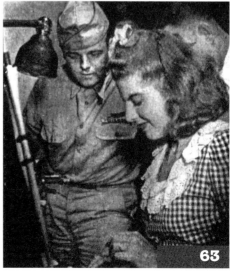

ADDRESSOGRAPH-MULTIGRAPH CORPORATION

· General Offices ·
1200 BABBITT ROAD, EUCLID, OHIO

TELEPHONE: KENMORE 4800
CABLE ADDRESS: Addmulcor

July 15, 1943

Miss Margaret Polk
1095 Poplar Avenue
Memphis, Tennessee

My dear Miss Polk:

Thursday, July 8th, was such a busy day for all of us! I do hope it was a happy day for you -- and that you and Bob also found full enjoyment in the days immediately following.

When your mother told me Friday that you had decided to go to Dayton, I knew that you would have a few more precious hours with him.

Yours must have been a great thrill on learning of Bob's promotion to the rank of Major.

While you were in Dayton, Mr. Powers and I had a most interesting time trying to follow up the origin of the "they are going to get married in Cleveland" story carried in the Cleveland Plain Dealer on Friday morning, July 9th. Unfortunately, we did not get to the bottom of the plot - if such it was - but we did find that the Plain Dealer had made pretty elaborate arrangements. They were all ready with all the trimmings necessary to a wedding. As you probably already know, both your and Bob's denials were carried in all Cleveland papers.

Now that you are again back home and settled into the usual daily routine, I hope you and your mother get your heads together right away and let me know the amount of incidental expenses incurred by you and her in making the trip. The transportation and hotel bill have been taken care of, I know, but there are always other items - and, as I told you over the phone a few weeks ago, you were to be our guests. Please let me make good completely on that invitation in behalf of the corporation.

We are still busy with the aftermath of the rally. The printer is today picking up material for a pictorial souvenir edition of the Memphis Belle rally of our A-M NEWS. It should be off the press within a week or ten days. We shall send you several copies. If they do not reach, just let us know and we shall send you more.

We also hope to get together many of the photographs taken during the rally. As soon as we get prints of them, I shall send them on to you.

All of us did enjoy the presence of you and your mother at the rally and I do hope that you enjoyed to the full the all-too-short visit you had with Bob.

With warmest personal regards, believe me

Sincerely

Henry Metz

Advertising Manager

HLMetz:r

Tales of Bob Morgan's antics behind the scenes are somewhat lurid so that without too much 'reading between the lines' it is clear that a good time and lots of fun was to be had by all. There were the girls in the factories, girls in the hospitality suites, girls along the parade routes, girls at cocktail parties, dinners and receptions... and almost certainly in hotel rooms. As Bob Morgan once said *'We were boys in uniform and the newspapers and radio stations had told them we had done something special and they treated us that way. And we accepted it'.*

In Euclid there another girl - this one not discreetly 'supplied', but one firmly pushed out by the Public Relations people. Margaret Polk and her mother had been secretly flown up from Memphis to appear on stage just as Bob Morgan had finished his crew introductions to the gathered thousands. The crowd went wild.

A view of just some of the crowds awaiting the arrival of the crew of the *Memphis Belle* at the Addressograph-Multigraph Corp facility in Euclid.

The *Memphis Belle's* Grand Tour of America cannot be told without including the story and background to the break-up of Bob Morgan and Margaret Polk's relationship which occurred during the latter stages of the tour and has therefore, been slotted in with the timeline. After all, if it was not for Margaret, there would have been no *Memphis Belle*.

The tour would also be difficult for a number of the crew, in that they had to 'toe the party line' for they were now part of the 25 mission crew story as put out by the propagandists within the Army Air Force. It would be especially difficult for Jim Verinis, for it would be the start of living in Bob Morgans 'shadow' - something he did for the rest of his life - when the Press eternally dubbed him as the *Memphis Belle's* copilot. This was despite the fact that he had commanded *Connecticut Yankee* for twenty missions AND beat Bob Morgan to the magic twenty-five missions completed!

The Tour was to sell war bonds - it was also about keeping the public and war-workers on the side of the Air Force who at the time was fighting on three fronts - in Europe, in the Pacific and in Congress! Public interest was phenomenal, as was shown by the thousands who turned out at each stop of the tour!

Despite what many have claimed over the years, it is clear that after making a number of sweeps over Dayton, all the local newspapers of the day report that the *Memphis Belle* touched down on Patterson Field - not Wright - at 1pm that Friday. Patterson Field is to the east of Wright Field, now the home of the National Museum of the Air Force, to be greeted by some 6,000 Air Service Command (ASC) employees and Army officers. For the record, the two fields were amalgamated under the name Wright-Patterson Air Force Base in 1948.

However, there was just as much if not more interest in the potential forthcoming nuptials between the dashing Captain pilot and his fiance, for the rumours from Cleveland had gotten to Dayton before them!

After a brief ceremony of welcome by Major-General Walter H Frank, the head of ASC, Colonel M .G. Estabrook, Commander of Fairfield Air Service Command, Colonel J. A. Woodruff, Commander of Patterson Field and Mayor Frank Krebs, there was a big surprise for Bob Morgan. During the welcoming ceremony, Major General Frank surprised him by pinning on a set of oak leaves borrowed from Major Henry M Paynter, thus promoting Captain Morgan to Major Morgan!

Following the noon rally at Patterson Field, they all adjourned to the Wilbur Wright Officers Club for lunch, where each member of the crew were presented with $100 worth of war bonds and a Bulova Aviation Watch given by Arola Bulova, a personal friend of General Frank and head of the Bulova Watch Co. According to reports, J S Sussman, agent for Bulova Watches said that seven more watches would be set aside for the Groundcrew when they returned from Bassingbourn. Two special guests at the luncheon were the parents of Bill Winchell.

Both the *Dayton Daily News* and the *Dayton Journal* described that the aircraft and crew had arrived for a curtailed two day visit - it seems that the original plan was for a three-day stop-over, but that it had been cut short for as the *News* said *'the crew will leave at 9am Sunday for the east where they*

Opposite page: two views taken after the *Memphis Belle's* arrival at Patterson Field, just outside of Dayton, OH. The pictures gives some idea as to the crowd who attended this, and other events.

In the picture above, Bob Morgan in front of the crowd at Patterson Field. 'WING' on the banner attached to his microphone stand refers to Dayton radio station WING who broadcast the event from the field. On the platform also can be seen the crew, local dignitaries and Major General Walter H Frank.

The pictures gives some idea as to the crowd who attended this, and other events.

Bill Winchell's parents, along with Major General Walter H Frank. watch Bob Morgan throw the *Memphis Belle* around over the skies above Patterson Field before landing.

Below: the happy reunion. Bill's parents had driven down from Chicago.

will confer with Air Force Officers'. The *Journal* went on to describe that *'The 'Memphis Belle and her members will get complete 'checkovers' during their two-day stay at Patterson Field beginning today. Officials for the Air Service Command said Patterson Field mechanics will completely overhaul the Flying Fortress after it arrives. Likewise, crew members, two of whom who have not been 'feeling up to par' will be examined by physicians at the field's post hospital'.*

Certainly the aircraft 'checkover' is borne out by the maintenance logs which shows that the *Memphis Belle* caught up with the outstanding fifty and one hundred hour maintenance checks whilst at Dayton. This was also borne out by Irene Somers, who worked first-hand on the aircraft while it was there. *'It was war, and most of the men in my family was in it, so I decided I would join too. I signed up, passed the exam and went to work as a mechanic. I was always a tom-boy, and became just one of the guys. They treated me fine. And they were the ones who gave me my nickname of Suzie-Q. One of them could not remember the name Irene, so he called me that and it kind of stuck'.*

Irene's speciality was working with Plexiglass - heating and shaping it to fit aircraft windows and doors. While working at Patterson Field, her boss called her to one side. *'He told me to get my tools - there was something special he wanted me to do. He knew that everyone knew the Memphis Belle was at Patterson Field and that they'd all want to work on it, so he was going to keep it real quiet. We got special passes to wash and repair the plane's windows'.*

When the crew arrived at the Biltmore Hotel, they discovered another surprise - they learned that everything was on the house with the National Cash Register Co. picking up all the bills, for the rooms, the entertainment and any and all long-distance telephone calls that the wished to make! That evening they were entertained in the Biltmore's famous Kitty Hawk Room.

The next day was another busy one for the crew. In the morning they visited the National Cash Register Co. and the Standard Register Co. On stage at the NCR was Colonel E A Deeds, chairman of the Board, along with pioneer aviator Orville Wright and Major General Lester T Miller chief of the supply division ASC. Radio station WHIO broadcast from the NCR auditorium, and rebroadcast a transcription later that day. In the meantime, the aircraft was moved over to the Dayton Municipal Airport at Vandalia, where it was on display to the public from 1 to 9 pm.

There were to be two Bond Rallies, one with a parade through downtown Dayton to the courthouse steps with the crew arriving at 11.30 am, and the other out at the airport, where the Patterson Field Band played. One gimmick was to give out photographs of the crew to anyone that made a $1,000 purchase at the War Bond Rally.

While the crew were fetéd in Dayton, the aircraft got a long-overdue overhaul. Irene Somers was a mechanic specialising in aircraft windows. She is seen in the main picture standing half out of the Pilot's window of the *Memphis Belle* when it underwent maintenance at Patterson Field Ohio in July 1943.

Irene - known as Suzie-Q - is also seen in the picture on the right, second from the right, helping to shape a piece of plexiglas.

STANDARD REGISTER COMPA

Welcome MEN OF THE "MEMPHIS BELLE"

DAYTON, OHIO, JULY 10, 1943

Above: Banners and bunting welcome the crew to the Standard Register Company - as appearing in the company newsletter of July 10 1943.

Left: Left to right: Bob Morgan and Jim Verinis get to meet aviation pioneer Orville Wright and Colonel E A Deeds, Chairman of the National Cash Register Company.

Below: Bob Morgan and the crew on stage in the NCR Auditorium. The decoration on the curtain behind clearly represents the aircraft nose art.

Cleveland OH to Dayton OH - 9th July
Flight time: one hour fifteen minutes.

Dayton OH to Las Vegas NV - 11th July
Flight time: ten hours

Little has been located regarding the arrival of the crew at Las Vegas Army Air Field - much later to be re-named and expanded as Nellis AFB, although it is known they stayed at the then recently-opened Hotel Last Frontier.

During this same time, Basic Magnesium Inc. (BMI) operated a magnesium plant just outside Las Vegas to help in the war effort. Magnesium was used for such items as tyre rims, bullets, bombs and planes. At the time, the area was called 'Basic Townsite', but was renamed Henderson in 1944.

The plant began making magnesium in August 1942 and most of the workers at the plant were women. In just over two years, the plant produced 166 thousand tons of magnesium.

July 12th 1943 saw the crew making a full day visit to the BMI, having been assigned a fleet of cars to take them around the massive complex. The occasion was to mark the completion of the last huge unit that put the plant into full production. Just after noon, the guests were taken for lunch at Anderson's Camp before continuing the tour. That evening a parade was mounted, the description of which today shows just how different Las Vegas and the surrounding area was then!

The parade formed at Water Street and Basic Road at the Townsite before proceeding down Water Street to Anderson's camp and the Trailer Park. The Las Vegas Army Air Field Band led the procession, which concluded with ceremonies at the baseball field near Gate One. Mechanised equipment from the airfield and Camp Williston, a Boulder City based camp for training Army Guards, formed part of the parade line up with the *Memphis Belle* crew occupying places on prominence in the line of march. Managing Editor of the *Las Vegas Review-Journal* John Cahlan was selected as master of ceremonies for the event, with speakers Lieutenant-Colonel P O Brewer, Commander of the 52nd Sub Depot Air Service Command and Gordon Reid of the War Department as well as the *Memphis Belle* crew addressing the war workers.

These pages show the aircraft and crew at Las Vegas, inlcuing pictures of their bisit to Basic Magnesium.

The crew, along with Mr F O Case, the General Manager of Basic Magnesium Inc at McCarren Field, Las Vegas. The label on the presentation ingot reads *'From Basic Magnesium to Berlin (via the Memphis Belle)*

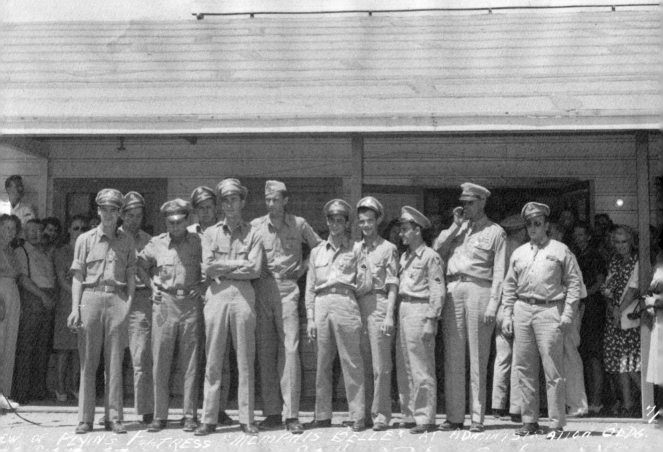

BASIC MAGNESIUM

Kingman Army Air Field and Bob Morgan sweeps the *Memphis Belle* in low over the runway. Interestingly, close study of the original print suggests that the port outer prop appears to be feathered. *[via Harry Friedman]*

The *Mohave County Miner* for Thursday July 15th clearly states that the *Memphis Belle* and crew arrived at Kingman on the 14th, the aircraft itself bears contradictory evidence, for scratched into the skin is '*Leonard Nelson, Kingman - July 13 1943*'. which strongly suggests that the aircraft was at Kingman on July 13th.

When the *Memphis Belle* and crew arrived at Kingman, Arizona, apart from visiting with the servicemen out at Kingman Army Air Field, the crew met with the townsfolk. They were introduced by Lieutenant Alfred B McCreary, public relations officer from Kingman, but we shall let the *Mohave County Minor* newspaper pick up the story.

Under the headline *"Memphis Belle" Crew Guests of Rotary, Lions at Luncheon Meet, Wed.* the article started with the sub heading of *Relate interesting incidents of combat missions over German held territory to interested audience.* It continued: '*Probably the largest group of Rotarians and Lions ever together in Kingman were on hand at their joint meeting last Wednesday noon in the Methodist Church basement. Most welcome feature of the meeting was the pleasure that the two service clubs had in being hosts to the gallant crew of the "Memphis Belle" recently back from dropping bombs on Germany and German-occupied countries to make a tour of the United States. With the exception of the bombardier, who was otherwise occupied and unable to be in attendance, the crew which met with the two clubs was the same one which left the United States last year to engage in combat with the minions of Hitler*'.

Las Vegas NV to Kingman AZ - July 13th
Flight time: one hour fifteen minutes.

Kingman AZ - July 14th
Flight time: one hour.

Kingman AZ to Roswell NM - July 15th
Flight time: three flights, totalling four hours thirty minutes.

Roswell NM to Hobbs NM - July 16th
Flight time: one hour.

Hobbs NM to San Antonio TX - July 17th
Flight time: two hours fifteen minutes.

The site at Roswell was acquired in 1941 by the USAAF for the purpose of establishing a Military Flying Training Center and Bombardier School. Although there was a bombing target adjacent to the runway, the only items dropped from an aircraft were bags of sand or flour. The practice bombing and gunnery ranges were due south of the airfield.

Likewise Hobbs Army Air Base was an aviation training facility that mostly trained B-17 pilots for service overseas and was in the general direction of their next known stop at San Antonio, Texas. Hobbs is a straight-line distance of 90 miles from Roswell, about the right time for the journey plus a Morgan 'display' at the arrival at Hobbs. This also makes sense of the flight time for the next day, July 17th, for the 350 mile straight-line distance would be comfortably accomplished by the two-hour fifteen minute flight.

Plans for the forthcoming arrival of the *Memphis Belle* in San Antonio started at least

San Antonio Welcomes the

MEMPHIS BELLE
and Her Gallant Crew

Hear the Story
of the
MEMPHIS BELLE
at the
AUDITORIUM
Tonight at
8:30

"I Will Look to the Heavens From Whence Cometh My Help"

To the crews of the planes like the Memphis Belle we owe our thanks for the wonderful progress our fighting forces have made. Every day they unhesitatingly offer their lives that you and I and our children may continue to enjoy the freedom that for 167 years has been ours.

Today, the eyes of the Allied nations and the oppressed, occupied countries of Europe are turned skyward in expectancy and hope. Justice will be dealt from the heavens. Out of fleecy cloudbanks, out of storm swept skies, out of the blackness of the night and the sun-flooded hours of the day will come the Delivering Angel in the form of Allied air power.

Let us help speed that day when victory will be ours. And let's speed it by the *continuous, uninterrupted* purchase of War Bonds. Let's not call our responsibility ended merely because we possess one crisp twenty-five dollar bond—or a dozen—or a hundred. Let's not forget that a mighty force for freedom lies in every bond that we buy. . . .

Let's put that force to work.

BY BUYING MORE WAR BONDS

THE BIG WHITE
FURNITURE STORE

a week before with discussions between Mayor Gus B. Mauermann and Major Edward Burns of Kelly Field. The aircraft was to be displayed at Alamo Airport on Sunday and then at Stinson Field the next day. Every day *The San Antonio Light* newspaper contained more and more detail as to the plans, working the public up into a greater and greater frenzy.

At 3pm Bob Morgan touched down at Kelly Field to start the three-day celebrations in their honor after making a number of low passes over the airfield. The proceedings were broadcast 'as they happened' by radio station KABC when Major Edward J Burns, Chaplain of the San Antonio Air Service Command, introduced the crew to the gathered 20,000 workers.

At 5pm the military organisations at Kelly Field honoured the crew with a formal military review, the salute being taken by by Major Morgan for his men. Then it was off to the Plaza Hotel, where C W Miller, the manager of Sears Roebuck, was picking up the tab.

Sunday was a day of rest, but shortly after noon, three crew members ferried the *Memphis Belle* from Kelly Field to the San Antonio Municipal Airport to put the aircraft on display for the public. Monday saw a big parade forming up at the Auditorium Circle in downtown San Antonio - the scale and detail of it all deserves repeating here, for it shows just how importantly this tour was being taken, but then, we guess they do things big in Texas!

Head of the parade was a police escort, followed by the official cars, general officers, city officials, commanding officers of posts, honourary foreign nationals and visiting city officials. Organisations from Kelly Field came next headed by their band, followed by the troops, WAACs and civilians from the Engineering department. Then came the San Antonio Aviation Cadet Center with their band, troops and WAACs. The American Legion Post along with the local VFW came next, with the crew of the *Memphis Belle* slotted in between the Yanks, Cowboys and chuck-wagon. They were, however, each provided with a Jeep with their name on it and a driver! There followed on the units from Stinson Field with their band, troops weapons carriers, the Brooks Field Band, the Hondo School of Navigation and the Lasso Girls from Jefferson High School. Numerous city clubs were also invited to march, the route being from the Auditorium Circle, south on to Jefferson Street, west on Houston Street to Soledad Street to south of Soledad Street to Commerce Street east on Commerce Street to Alamo, north on Alamo to Houston Street. At the Alamo Plaza the parade paused to allow Major Morgan to lay a wreath at the cenotaph on behalf of all the crewmembers. This was followed by a big gathering in the Municipal Auditorium that evening for the populace to listen to the crews exploits.

Another day, and another destination - the *Memphis Belle* arrived overhead the Harlingen Army Air Field with an airborne escort of AT-6 Texan trainers to participate in their 'Buy a Fighter Plane' drive. Amongst the reception committee on the ground was Colonel John R. Morgan, Commanding Officer of the field.

After arrival the crew toured the airfield and Sub Depot, making addresses to the employees there. The aircraft meanwhile was parked just inside the South Gate on Rio Hondo Road, with a special walkway and platform constructed over one wing so as to allow the public to see through the aircraft windows and was on display until sundown both days. That evening there was an all-Army talent show given by HAAF entertainers at the Fair Park Auditorium during which the crew appeared on stage.

Two views of the *Memphis Belle* being made ready (above) and then on display (left) to the public at Harlingen, Texas with the specially constructed 'platform over one wing so the public could see inside. *[via Harry Friedman]*

The *Memphis Belle* arrived over Laredo and Morgan circled the city a few times before touching down at the Laredo Army Air Field at 1.30pm in front of US and Mexican dignitaries and thousands of gunnery

On arrival, Bob Morgan was asked to make his usual presentation of the crew and speech, which this time was broadcast over KPAB. Shortly afterwards, and headed by an escort provided by the local police department, the crew were convoyed to Nuevo Laredo, where in front of the Federal Building they were greeted by General Silvestre Pinal Villabueva and his staff along with representatives if the city, state and federal government.

Right: Thought to have been taken in the Cadillac Bar, Nuevo Laredo, General Silvestre Pinal Villabueva, centre, has a beer with Bob Morgan.

Below: the most transient of documents as anyone who has ever had anything to do with the military will know, is the infamous 'temporary pass' - so it is truly remarkable that we have John Quinlans 'ticket to Mexico'!

LAREDO ARMY AIR FIELD
TEMPORARY MEXICO PASS.

11:00 PM
EXPIRES 23 July 43

Quinlan, John P.   Staff Sergeant   Tail Gunner "Memphis Belle"
SURNAME   FIRST   MIDDLE   RANK   ASN   ORGANIZATION   CODE.
is granted the privilege of visiting the City of Nuevo Laredo, Mexico
in uniform, when not on duty. Bearer to return to the U. S. side not
later than 11:00 P. M. (CWT) on the day of the Visit.

NOT IN EXCESS OF THE ALLOWED 15%:

WILBUR H. GREENSTREET,
Commanding.
1st. Lt., Air Corps,
Provost Marshal

REGULATIONS COVERING MILITARY PERSONNEL VISITING NUEVO LAREDO, MEXICO:

1. The only U. S. Money allowed in Mexico is $2.00 bills and silver.
2. Return across the bridge before 11:00 P. M. (CWT). Do not go by
Mexico time; it is an hour earlier than U. S. time.
3. The visiting of Nuevo Laredo, Mexico is a privilege. Anyone abu-
sing the privilege by crossing the bridge late, or conducting themselves
in such a way as to bring discredit to the Service, will lose the privilege. It is the bearer's responsibility to see that his name is taken
by the M. P.'s as he crosses the bridge and also to have it checked off
as he returns.
4. I have read the above regulations and understand them.

(Signature)

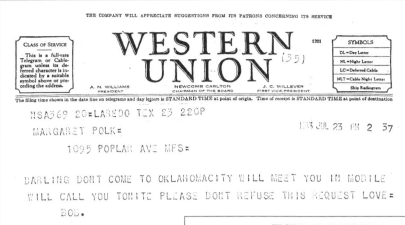

Left: Bob's telegram to Margaret changing some arrangements.

THE COMPANY WILL APPRECIATE SUGGESTIONS FROM ITS PATRONS CONCERNING ITS SERVICE

WESTERN UNION

CLASS OF SERVICE
This is a full-rate Telegram or Cablegram unless its deferred character is indicated by a suitable symbol above or preceding the address.

A. N. WILLIAMS
PRESIDENT

NEWCOMB CARLTON
CHAIRMAN OF THE BOARD

J. C. WILLEVER
FIRST VICE-PRESIDENT

1201 (35)

SYMBOLS
DL = Day Letter
NL = Night Letter
LC = Deferred Cable
NLT = Cable Night Letter
Ship Radiogram

The filing time shown in the date line on telegrams and day letters is STANDARD TIME at point of origin. Time of receipt is STANDARD TIME at point of destination

HSA369 20=LAREDO TEX 23 220P

MARGARET POLK=

1095 POPLAR AVE MFS=

1943 JUL 23 PM 2 37

DARLING DONT COME TO OKLAHOMACITY WILL MEET YOU IN MOBILE
WILL CALL YOU TONITE PLEASE DONT REFUSE THIS REQUEST LOVE=

BOB.

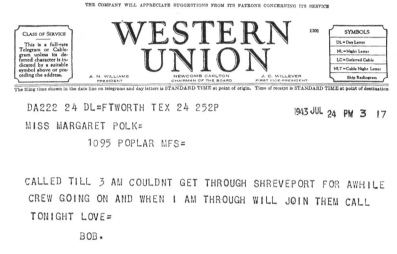

Right: The content of this telegram is not as important as where is was sent from - Fort Worth, Texas. It's another minor item to suggest that the crew did visit there during the tour.

THE COMPANY WILL APPRECIATE SUGGESTIONS FROM ITS PATRONS CONCERNING ITS SERVICE

WESTERN UNION

CLASS OF SERVICE
This is a full-rate Telegram or Cablegram unless its deferred character is indicated by a suitable symbol above or preceding the address.

A. N. WILLIAMS
PRESIDENT

NEWCOMB CARLTON
CHAIRMAN OF THE BOARD

J. C. WILLEVER
FIRST VICE-PRESIDENT

1201

SYMBOLS
DL = Day Letter
NL = Night Letter
LC = Deferred Cable
NLT = Cable Night Letter
Ship Radiogram

The filing time shown in the date line on telegrams and day letters is STANDARD TIME at point of origin. Time of receipt is STANDARD TIME at point of destination

DA222 24 DL=FTWORTH TEX 24 252P

MISS MARGARET POLK=

1095 POPLAR MFS=

1943 JUL 24 PM 3 17

CALLED TILL 3 AM COULDNT GET THROUGH SHREVEPORT FOR AWHILE
CREW GOING ON AND WHEN I AM THROUGH WILL JOIN THEM CALL
TONIGHT LOVE=

BOB.

That evening they were entertained by local civilians at the Cadillac Bar in Nuevo Laredo where Claude Fullick acted as Master of Ceremonies. Later they were visitors at John O'Hern's 'Big O' ranch.

The aircraft was parked adjacent to the Country Club where thousands of Laredoans inspected it under the watchful eye of Major Tom Lane, the Commander of the 388th Sub Depot who was in charge of the arrangements. Major Lane stressed to the Press that the aircraft and crew were NOT in Laredo to sell War Bonds, although there would be a booth at the Country Club, staffed by members of the Webb Country War Bond Committee of which Mrs Albert Martin was the chairman. It seems that the Committee - in the shape of Miss Suzy Neel and Miss Ruth Annette Neel - sold some $2,014.00 worth of bonds and stamps from a booth set up under the wing of the *Memphis Belle*.

The next day - Friday July 23rd - the crew paraded through the city, each member aboard a Jeep bearing his name. The parade finished at the Jarvis Plaza, where again each crew member was introduced to the crowd. Before leaving on Saturday morning tailgunner John Quinlan managed to find time to address the graduating class from the Laredo Gunnery School!

From Laredo it was on to Fort Worth TX - a stop of which very little is known - before heading to the first of a pair of 'big ones' - Oklahoma.

Cecil Scott speaks to the gathered crowds at the Oklahoma City Air Deport - how do we know the location...? The microphone in front of him shows WKYA, one of the Oklahoma City Radio Stations!

San Antonio TX to Harlingen, TX - July 20th
Flight time: two hours.

Harlingen to Laredo, TX - July 22nd
Flight time one hour thirty minutes.

Laredo TX to Forth Worth TX - July 24th
Flight time: three hours forty-five minutes

Forth Worth TX to Oklahoma City - July 25th
Flight time: one hour.

Oklahoma City to Cheyenne - July 27th
Flight time: five hours.

Cheyenne to Denver CO - July 29th
Flight time: one hour thirty minutes.

Denver CO to Wichita KA - August 1st
Flight time: four hours.

The huge Oklahoma City Air Depot - the largest installation of its kind in the country and rumoured to have cost $30,000,000 in 1943 - was to be opened to the public for the first time to co-incide with the arrival of the *Memphis Belle* and crew. Also known as Tinker Army Air Field, the Depot was commanded by Brigadier General Arthur W. Vanaman who was quoted prior to the visit as saying *'The Belle's visit will be one of four major stops for her crew in a nationwide tour. It makes me very happy to have received permission to have an open house for the public. The Army Air Force is very proud of our layout here - it is a model depot - we know Oklahoma City and Oklahoma area and we want the public to come out here and see what is here'.*

It would be many of the local public's first chance at seeing the USAAF at close quarters. On display would be Flying Fortesses, Liberators, Havocs and other bombers and pursuit ships, as would be a Douglas Skytrain cargo carrier assembled at the local Douglas plant. It was expected that some 50,000 would turn up at the field, in temperatures expected to reach 102 degrees Fahrenheit.

Come the day, Bob Morgan took the *Memphis Belle* on the by-now-usual circular tour of the city before landing, this time at 2pm. The response to the opening of the Depot and their arrival was incredible - it was estimated that over 115,000 people passed through the gates between 12.00 and 5.30pm when it closed - and it was in the 103+ degree-heat!

The *Memphis Belle* and her crew breezed into Cheyenne for the start of that city's five-day 'Frontier Days' show, the world's largest rodeo celebrations. That morning's *The Wyoming Eagle - Cheyenne* told that free photographs of the aircraft and crew would be given to War Bond buyers, even offering 'war-buggy' rides to prospective purchasers! Free Jeep rides to the 47th Frontier Days show were to be served up to eager Cheyenne war bond buyers - all they had to do was call radio station KFBC and a 'war-buggy' would arrived at the callers home to take them to either the airport or Frontier Park to make their purchase and claim their picture. During World War Two the airport served as a completion and modification center for B-17 aircraft. The tail turret fitted on later models of the B-17 became known as the 'Cheyenne' turret because it was developed at the modification and completion center there.

KFBC flashed news of the *Memphis Belle's* arrival at 4pm, the aircraft then being parked at the United Air Lines Care and Maintenance base, their hosts for the visit. The crew were met by UAL officials, members of the Frontier Days committee, local and state officials along with top-ranking Army officers before being taken to the Frontier Days Park. That evening United Air Lines hosted a reception and dinner in honor of the crew at the Plains Hotel in downtown Cheyenne.

Wednesday in Cheyenne was declared 'War Workers Day' and at 10am the crew participated by riding in a stagecoach in the United Air Lines section. It was then to the UAL modification centre for lunch and an address to the workers before heading to the Frontier Park in the

Bob Morgan and the crew in Cheyenne, along with 'Miss War Worker' and her two 'Maids of Honor'.
[via Harry Friedman]

OFFICIAL PROGRAM

"THE DADDY OF 'EM ALL"

EDWARD T. STOREY, Announcer   JOHN BELL, Arena Director

1943 FRONTIER DAYS COMMITTEE

R. J. HOFMANN, Chairman

JAMES A. STOREY, Treasurer
F. B. McVICAR, Indians
CHARLES J. HUGHES, Parade

W. A. NORRIS, Tickets
LT. COL. E. J. ZIMMERMAN, Military
DR. D. W. McENERY, Military

R. D. HANESWORTH, Secretary

ARENA OFFICIALS:
John Bell
Ed McCarty
Paul Hanson
Chas. Hirsig
B. Hirsig

TRACK OFFICIALS:
W. J. Dinneen
C. A. Black
James A. Buchanan
F. H. Porter

OFFICIAL TIMERS:
Wm. F. DeVere
George Storey
T. Blake Kennedy
F. W. Fitch

CLERK OF COURSE:
C. N. Bloomfield
State Veterinarian
Dr. H. D. Port

OFFICIAL STARTER:
Chas. N. Crain

PROGRAM AND CONTESTANTS:
Dan E. Rees

ARENA JUDGES:
Doff Aber
Shirley Hussey
Tim Bernard

Live stock for this show furnished by J. C. Sorensen, Camas, Idaho; Elliott and Nesbit, Cheyenne, Wyo.
Public Address System by Oliver W. Frey, Cheyenne, Wyoming

Second Day of Show, Wednesday, July 28, 1943

Event No. 1—GRAND OPENING ENTRY AND PARADE OF CONTESTANTS.

Event No. 2—CALF RIDING FOR BOYS UNDER 16 YEARS OF AGE. Fifteen riders each day. No entrance fee.

Dick Pickett
Robert Wallin
Ivan Peterman
Melvin Federer
Robert Apodaca

Roy E. Butler
Lawrence Barry
Richard Magor
Richard Deets
Dorrance Stratham

Walter Patterson
Raymond Benson
Rudy Apodaca
Manuel Renteria
Johnny Sanchez

Event No. 3—CEREMONIAL BATTALION PARADE, BY TROOPS FROM THE RE-PLACEMENT CENTER, FORT FRANCIS E. WARREN. Major Earl R. Otis, Commanding, Captain Kelton S. Lynn, Adjutant. QMRTC troops from Company A and C of the 5th Regiment, and Company D of the 2nd Regiment.
TRICK DRILL SQUADS. One squad from each QMRTC Regiment.

SPECIAL EVENT—Presentation of World Famous "Memphis Belle" Flying Fortress Crew, "Miss War Worker," and Maids of Honor.

Event No. 4—Out of Chutes. BRAHMA STEER RIDING CONTEST. Purse $1,400.00 and all entrance fees. Entrance fee $10.00. Purse will be divided into two day moneys of 30 per cent each and divided 40, 30, 20 and 10 per cent. Final money, or the remaining 40 per cent of the purse divided 40, 30, 20 and 10 per cent. Trophies: Winner to receive a silver belt buckle through the Frontier Hotel, Cheyenne, Wyoming.

13. Ernie King on S-110
29. S. A. York on S-11
44. Fred Badsky on S-33
74. Gerald Roberts on S-28
81. Marvin Shoulders on S-4
95. George Fletcher on S-10
108. Lowell Ford on S-44
111. Bill Maxey on E-5
112. Bob Burrows on S-3
113. Robt. Stetler on E-13

116. Jack Gray on E-2
134. Red Billingsley on S-1
138. Bob Estes on E-17
139. Jack Couch on E-79
148. Art Casteel on E-52
165. Orville Stanton on E-1
173. Wayne Ewing on E-87
203. Freckles Brown on S-16
217. Fritz Becker on E-50
222. Virgil Earp on S-14

Event No. 5—In Arena. First Section WORLD'S CHAMPIONSHIP CALF ROPING CONTEST. Purse $1,400.00 and all entrance fees. Entrance fee $50.00. This purse to be divided into two day moneys of 30 per cent each and divided 40, 30, 20 and 10 per cent. Final money or the remaining 40 per cent of the purse to be divided 40, 30, 20 and 10 per cent. Unless the roper makes a catch with the first rope, he must throw both loops before retiring to indicate that he is through. Trophies: Winner to receive saddle through Montgomery Ward Company of Cheyenne, Wyoming, and a silver and gold belt buckle through the Plymouth Cordage Company of North Plymouth, Mass.

20. Bill Maycock
49. John Bowman
55. Jeff Good
62. Morris Laycock
70. Buck Goodspeed
77. George Richmond

83. Buck Sorrells
86. Hugh Clingman
89. Jack Skipworth
93. Jack Sanders
96. J. K. Harris
100. Fox O'Callaghan

114. John Pogue
115. Pat Henry
127. Ray Barnes
136. Irby Mundy

CONCESSION PRICES

Beer	.20	Pop Corn	.10	Cigarettes	.20
Sandwiches	.20	Ice Cream	.10	Coffee	.10
Pop	.10			Cushions	.15

company of 'Miss War Worker' and her maids of honour for the opening ceremonies, rodeo and military review. *The Wyoming Eagle - Cheyenne* recorded that *'To a man, the crew of the Flying Fortress 'Memphis Belle', heroes of 25 missions over Nazi-dominated Europe and Germany, yesterday expressed their willingness to make a 26th flight over Axis country sooner than mounting a bucking bronco performing in Frontier Days'.*

The *Memphis Belle* touched down at the Denver Municipal Airport at 10.30am, having spent the previous twenty minutes being thrown around the sky over the city and airport by Bob Morgan. On hand to meet and greet the crew were Mayor Stapleton; Brigadier General Albert L Sneed, Commanding General of Lowry Field; Ralph A. Nicholas, state administrator of the war savings staff; Captain Jerry Toblin, Adjutant to the Denver Recruiting and Induction Center; Captain Aubrey Cookman, Public Relations Officer for Lowry Field; Lt. Thomas Tobias, Fourth District Army Air Force Training Command Public Relations Officer and Lt. Thelma J. Thompson WAC Recruiting Officer. Listed as also being on board the *Memphis Belle* was Captain Rodney L. Southwick, a public relations officer in charge of all publicity for the aircraft. It seems that he had flown down with the crew from Cheyenne.

Leaving the aircraft on display to the public between Gates 6 and 7 at the airport, the crew were taken to the Brown Palace Hotel and a noon luncheon as guests of the Denver Rotary Club and a public reception at the Denver Press Club from 5 to 7pm.

By the Friday morning, when the crew returned to the airport to taxi the aircraft over to the nearby aircraft modification centre ready to address the day shift at 12.30 an estimated 20,000 people had come out to the airport to see the *Memphis Belle*. The modification centre - operated by Continental Air Lines - was one of a number of plants where B-17s received final combat preparations. It was then back to the city for a War Bond Drive at Sixteenth and Champa Streets before returning back to the airport for the presentation of lapel buttons to aviation cadets reservists. Highlight of the evening for one cadet, 17 year-old Wilbur G. McFarland, was for him to be taken for a flight in the *Memphis Belle* which was broadcast live at 7pm on station KOA. Finally, the crew met and made speeches to the second and third shifts working at the modification centre.

According to the newspapers, the Saturday was an Army Air Force-ordered day of rest, but it seems that Denver was where Bob Morgan broke up with Margaret. It seems the crew were hosting a cocktail party at their hotel and Bob Morgan was to make his usual call to Margaret. She heard the sounds of the party going on in the background and asked him what was going on. Bob was forced to admit there was a party. At that point according to Bob Morgan a girl at the party tried to wrestle the receiver from him. Margaret was not amused. They had an argument and effectively broke up.

THE
"MEMPHIS BELLE"
BATTLE SCARRED FLYING FORTRESS
IS IN TOWN

Talk With a Member of Her
Crew at Rorabaugh-Buck's Monday,
12 o'Clock Until 1 P. M.
TEC. SGT. ROBERT J. HANSON

The Memphis Belle . . proud, battle scarred Flying Fortress is in town with her original crew of veteran young airmen after 25 history making raids over occupied France and Germany. One of her gallant members will be in our street floor bond booth tomorrow . . Monday from 12 o'clock until 1 p. m. He is Technical Sgt. Robert J. Hanson, the radio operator of the Memphis Belle, from Walla Walla, Washington. He handled the communications between and during battles . . manning a gun when necessary. He attributes the "Belle's" good fortune to his rabbit's foot that went on the 25 successful air raids.

Boeing PLANE TALK

BE SURE
TO TAKE YOUR BADGE
AND CARD
TO PARK MONDAY

READ CAREFULLY
"MEMPHIS BELLE"
PROGRAM INSTRUC-
TIONS ON PAGE 2

VOL. I   WICHITA, KANSAS, JULY 31, 1943   NO. 51

"MEMPHIS BELLE" AT PLANTS MONDAY

EMPLOYEES WILL HEAR B-17 CREW AT BOEING PARK

Boeing-Wichita employees of all three shifts will be given time off Monday afternoon and early Tuesday

THE LATEST DEVELOPMENT

We are indeed sorry to report that the progress of our application for wage increases is still "in the mill," and a continuation of our "play by play" description finds us with only the following information to add to that set out in last week's PLANE TALK:

"THE ANALYSIS OF OUR WAGE INCREASE REQUEST HAS BEEN

Below: Bob Morgan taxies the *Memphis Belle* past YB-29 41-36959 parked on the ramp at Boeing Witchita.

Below: An overall view of part of the Boeing Wichita Plant as workers stream back across the parking lot have been top have a look at the *Memphis Belle* visible in the centre of the picture. The supposedly 'highly secret YB-29' - and noticeable by its distinctive tail can be seen off to the left. *[via Harry Friedman]*

Above: Workers from the Boeing plant crowd around the *Memphis Belle*. It seems that some Boeing workers had their 'job description' embroidered on the back of their shirts

Left: The *Memphis Belle* crew are introduced to the workers at Boeing Wichita. *[both via Harry Friedman]*

THOUSANDS AT BOEING GREET "MEMPHIS BELLE" CREW

Newspaper articles - especially wartime newsprint - are notoriously difficult to reproduce with any degree of quality. Nevertheless, the cuttings from the Bond Tour make such fascinating reading for they show just how much attention was paid to the crew and the aircraft that such poor reproduction is worthwhile and can be accepted for the historical information they contain. This picture - take at Boeing Wichita - clearly shows just how much interest there was in the *Memphis Belle* and how much attention was showered upon her crew - for the time of the war bond tour, the crew were having a good war!

BOEING AIRPLANE COMPANY

WICHITA DIVISION

WICHITA, KANSAS

August 10, 1943

In Reply Refer to

JES:mkt
8/10/43

Maj. Gen. Ira C. Eaker
Headquarters VIII Bomber Command
A.P.O. 887
New York, New York

Dear Ira:

I hastily wrote you an informal note last week
to tell you how pleased and inspired we all were over the crew
of the Memphis Belle. Major Morgan and his officers and enlisted
men are doing a splendid job. They are to be commended and you
are to be highly complimented on your thoughtfulness in sending
these people to the United States on their 26th mission. They
are clean-cut, clear-eyed, two-fisted Americans and boy, they
tell their story so that it is not misunderstood.

Their visit made us all feel that it was a
distinct privilege to be a party to your outstanding successes.
With such men in your command and such equipment as we soon hope
to have in your hands, we can really expect knockout blows from
the VIII Bombardment Command as well as others throughout the world.

Our best wishes for continued success go with these
compliments to you and your splendid Command.

Sincerely and faithfully yours,

BOEING AIRPLANE COMPANY
Wichita Division

Vice President

JESchaefer:mkt
cc: Gen. H. H. Arnold
    Each member of Memphis Belle
    crew with copies of Boeing Planetalk

It seems that Boeing Wichita were very pleased with the conduct of the crew as this letter to Ira Eaker from the V-P of Boeing shows!

Break-up of a romance...

It was clear that the couple could not keep their romantic break-up concealed from the world for long. Sure enough, on Monday August 2nd Margaret spoke to someone, and it was picked up the next day as shown in the cutting below and flashed to other newspapers in the country.

> **Memphis Belle's Romance Ends.**
>
> Memphis, Aug. 2.—(AP.)—Remember the romance between the Flying Fortress pilot, Major Robert K. Morgan, and Margaret Polk for whom he named his plane "The Memphis Belle?"
>
> Well, says Miss Polk. It is ended. "There'll be no wedding," she asserted tonight. "But Bob and I will always be good friends." Refusing to disclose the reason, she said the engagement was broken by mutual agreement.

The next day another piece surfaced, revealing that Margaret had sent the engagement ring back to Bob the previous Saturday following a long-distance phone call.

Two days after that the piece on the right appeared - much less sympathetic, much more sarcastic, inferring the blame on Margaret in places. It's almost as if those following the Bob and Margaret romance were dividing into two camps!

Then, with a dateline of Asheville August 11, this paragraph appeared. Less that two weeks after breaking up from Margaret, Bob was announcing his engagement to Patricia Jane Huckins, the only daughter of Lt. Col Joseph Huckins, a girl he had met three weeks earlier in San Antonio!

Memphis Belle Brings Disillusionment To Pilot

It's almost certain there will never be another Flying Fortress named Memphis Belle. Not if Bob Morgan has anything to do with it. The original Memphis belle, Miss Margaret Polk, has just returned the engagement ring, together with one of those you-and-I-will-always-be-good-friends notes. So that's that.

Twenty-five times the Memphis Belle set out from the bomber base and headed for Hitlerland, each trip a victory. One needs only a little imagination to appreciate the thoughts that coursed through the mind of Pilot Morgan as he pointed the nose of the ship eastward. Bombs for Hitler . . . and each bomb bringing nearer the day that he other soldiers could get back to hometown belles all over the U. S. A.

Now, only disillusionment. Twenty-five trips in a good cause, to be sure, but the next 25 will not be made with the same zip and zest. What can the girl wish for, anyway? He's been promoted and now is Major Robert K. Morgan. He's a flier . . . a soldier . . . a brave man What does it take to thrill a girl's heart?

Of course, it is just possible that Morgan was the one that terminated the romance. We can't be sure. Still, from what we know of . . . Perhaps she has just heard of that fellow who dived a plane 780 miles an hour. He's a colonel, too. You never can tell!

At any rate, no more Memphis Belles. If the news gets around, there won't be any more like Sweet Sue, Bright Eyes, or Venus Girl, either. Poetry and romance will be expunged from Fortress christenings. We'll read about gallant deeds by Towser Boy, My Pal Joe, and Brooklyn Dodgers. The war will be won, but not in the adventurous spirit with which it started out.

'Memphis Belle' Pilot To Marry Texas Girl

Asheville. N. C., Aug. 11.—(AP.)—Major Robert K. Morgan, skipper of the famous Flying Fortress, "Memphis Belle," said here today he and Miss Patricia Jane Huckins of San Antonio, Texas, would be married next month.

Wherever the aircraft and crew went photographs were taken - but as the picture on the right shows - not everyone wanted or were happy to have their picture taken! Many found the usual state of 'wartime security' too great a contrast with the publicity and positive propaganda brought about by the war-bond tour.

Wichita KA to Mobile AL - August 3rd
Flight time: seven hours thirty minutes.

Mobile AL to Panama City FL - August 5th
Flight time: one hour forty-five minutes.

Panama City FL to Fort Myers FL - August 6th
Flight time: two hours thirty minutes.

Fort Myers FL to Hendricks Field Sebring FL - August 7th. Flight time: one hour.

The aircraft's arrival at Brookley Field in Mobile was scheduled for 2pm, with the thousands of employees at the Mobile Air Depot (MOAD) released from work for one hour to inspect the aircraft and listen to the crew. They in turn were welcomed by Brigadier General James A Mollison and then provided with a police motorcycle escort through the center of Mobile to the Admiral Semmes Hotel. Meanwhile, the public was allowed the view the aircraft out at the Brookley Field Air Depot on Cedar Point Road at Arlington Pier. The next day the crew travelled out to be presented at a private event at 2pm to the workers of the Aluminium Ore Company.

The arrival of the *Memphis Belle* is announced in the MOAD base newspaper.. *[via Harry Friedman]*

From Mobile, it was on to Tyndall Army Air Field. As early as July 17th the *Tyndall Target* was trumpeting that the *Memphis Belle* and crew would visit the airfield on August 5th. Tyndall Army Air Field, at Panama City, was used for gunnery training for Army bomber crews and arrangements for the visits were made by the 86th Sub-Depot Commanding Officer Major L. A. Byran.

Come the day, the first people in Panama City to see the *Memphis Belle* were a pair of Boy Scouts - William Cunmmin and Ira Lindsey - who were manning the observation platform on top of the Dixie Sherman Hotel. After landing, the crew were met by Acting Base Commander, Lt. Col. Jack L. Randolph, followed by brief speeches from Mayor Harry Fannin, Chamber of Commerce President George Longue and State Chamber of Commerce President Walter C. Sherman. As in so many other of the stops, a temporary radio station was set up at the field and the occasion was broadcast over WDLP.

Two pictures taken at Fort Meyers, Florida, as can be seen from the original caption marked on the negative.

Interestingly, both have been marked and dated '8-11-43' five days after the *Memphis Belle* and her crew visited - another verification example of how the US Base Photo Labs world-wide dated their images 'after the event'! *[both via Harry Friedman]*

Later in the day the crew addressed students at the aerial gunnery school and were honoured guests to dine at the Officers Club.

The remainder of the time around Florida - Sebring and Orlando - was uneventful - then it was to a very special location: Asheville, NC, Bob Morgan's home town! It was to be his homecoming. Bob Morgan brought the aircraft over Henderson-Asheville Airport at 10.30am after beating up the Biltmore Forest Country Club Golf Course. According to one of the local papers '...The Memphis Belle, bearing her scars with great grace and still growling her defiance, settled down on the north-south runway at the airport with a contented sigh, but defective brakes kept her racing the full length of the pavement and Morgan ran her off into the grass near the end'.

Morgan later admitted that he screwed up by not taking into account the lack of headwind, so he landed too fast and was forced to use the emergency brake and all his skill so as to miss a drainage ditch at the end - defective brakes indeed! Interestingly also, the Maintenance Log shows that Bob Morgan 'snagged' the brakes as not holding after the flight, but there is no record that the ground engineers did anything to fix them!

It was then photo-opportunity time before loading up a number of cars provided by the American Red Cross for a motorcade into the city, meeting up with the main parade at David Miller High School. The downtown parade disbanded at the Battery Park Hotel, where the crew would be headquartered for the duration of their stay. Meanwhile, the aircraft was parked in a large roped off area at the airport so the public could inspect it.

First item on the agenda in Asheville was a joint civil luncheon in the George Vanderbilt Hotel, then that evening there was a dinner held in their honour at the Grove Park Inn on Macon Avenue.

A pair of announcements from Ashville NC: above right: The announcement of the crew visit to America Enka Corp.

Right: A handbill from the Asheville 'Sky Club'

Next day it was to work, visiting a number of industrial plants. First on the schedule was Morgan Manufacturing at Black Mountain at 10am for an informal 'we're amongst friends' rally which after an opening address by Sgt C. M. DeYoung of the American Legion and prayers by Colonel Morgan Ashley, Chaplain of the Moore Military Hospital, Black Mountain attorney R. E. Finch delivered a welcome to the crew. They then went on to visit Beacon Manufacturing at Swannanoa, American Enka and the Sayles-Biltmore bleacheries.

That evening also saw another heavy schedule. First came a Reception at the Biltmore Forest Country Club, hosted by Bob Morgan's father David. At the reception desk of the Country Club sat a Dorothy Johnson. Dorothy was to make an more than a passing appearance in Bob Morgans life later. It was then on to the Courthouse for speeches to the Kiffin Rockwell post of the American Legion at 8.45pm. Already started was a public reception and Ball at the city auditorium with dancing to the Moore City Hospital Orchestra. Bob Morgan and his crew showed up there in time for a special 10.30pm radio broadcast by station WWNC. All indications are that from there they rounded off the evening with dancing at Johnny Rose's Sky Club.

This brings us to the matter of the infamous 'departure from Asheville'. Bob Morgan once described to us how, once they had taken off from Asheville, he decided that he would give the city one more show as a kind of 'farewell salute'. If his account is to be believed, it seems that he flew the *Memphis Belle* almost knife-edged - his own words '...at a sixty degree bank' between the Bumcombe County

Courthouse and the Asheville City Building that sat at the top of a gentle rise one side of Court Plaza at the head of Patton Evenue. The distance between the two building at ground level is just under 75 feet, opening up to 85 feet higher up!

According to Bob Morgan, the Weather Wing Unit of the Army Air Forces was housed in the City Hall at the time, and he was reported to the Pentagon for dangerous flying by the Unit's Lt Col. Commander - but nothing further was heard of the complaint due to the support Morgan is supposed to have had from General Arnold!

The only really modern picture in this book - but one that demonstrates where Bob Morgan took the Memphis Belle1. The Bumcombe County Courthouse Asheville NC is on the left - the Asheville City Building is on the right. The distance at the very top of the two buildings is 136 feet - lower down it reduces to 85 feet - and at ground level it is just 75 feet!
(Harry Friedman)

Above: While the crowds are kept at bay, Stuka goes for a quick run-around. Right: Waist Gunner Bill Winchell raids his Moms freezer in 639 Lower Humphrey.

Orlando FL to Asheville NC - August 11th
Flight time: three hours thirty minutes.

Asheville to Columbus OH - August 14th
Flight time: two hours thirty minutes.

Columbus OH to Chicago Il - August 15th
Flight time: two hours fifteen minutes.

Chicago to Salt Lake City - August 16th
Flight time: seven hours thirty minutes.

From Ashville NC the *Memphis Belle* and crew started the long trek out across the continent to Los Angeles.

The next stop was Lockbourne Army Air Base near Columbus OH. The primary unit at the base was the all-Black 447th Composite Group, also known as the Tuskegee Airmen.

The *Memphis Belle* and crew, according to the *Columbus Dispatch* '...swooped into Lockbourne Saturday for a two-day stop, the last on a mission that has taken the plane and crew to almost every air base in the country'.

They were met and greeted by Colonel Arthur C Foulk, Commanding Officer of the base and other officials. This stop was not for sightseeing. A program of lectures was scheduled at the Base Theater for officers and enlisted men aircrew and for men from the Sub-Depot.

After Columbus it was on to Chicago IL. Bill Winchell came home from the war to a welcome of a roast beef dinner and corn on the cob - and he used the *Memphis Belle* to do it! The aircraft and crew breezed in to the windy city and in the crowd to welcome them was Bill's mother Marion and his sister Mary. While Bill was whisked home, the rest of the crew were entertained by Lucien I Yoemans, a friend of Bob Morgan's father, at the famous Edgewater Beach Hotel. Here according to Morgan, he threw a party and introduced the crew to some girls.

The next morning, they were to visit an Air Power Exhibition in Tribune Square, sponsored by the Army Air Force's Materiel Command and *The Chicago Tribune*. On display in the Square - amongst other things - was a B-24 bomber and a P-47 fighter. According to the newspaper reports, after visiting the exhibition, it was then back to the hotel before heading out west again for Hollywood, with a scheduled stop at Salt Lake City.

Bob Morgan was later to claim this was the 'offical departure from Chicago - in reality it was somewhat different. As they were leaving the hotel, it seems that they were approached by a group of girls in Red Cross uniforms. The girls knew they were going to Los Angeles, and could they bum a lift? Morgan, it seems, said OK, despite it being against all the rules carry unauthorised passengers in a military aircraft.

After two hours of flying from Chicago, they 'threw a jug' on number 3 engine. The engine was shut down and the crew made a forced landing at 'Ogden Air Force Base'. It all sounds highly dramatic. The *Memphis Belle's* 'enforced' stopover at Ogden is told somewhat differently by the aircraft's maintenance log records. On August 16th 1943 there was a seven hour 30 minute flight and in the 'defects' column there is an entry that says *'#2 engine runs very rough'*. One has to query the sense of apparently flying on for five-and-a-half hours on three engines with a number of illegal passengers on board as Bob Morgan told the story - and as Ogden field is about 30 miles from Salt Lake City, was there not a closer airfield they could make a 'forced landing' at during that five-and-a-half hours?

Ogden Air Depot to Los Angeles Mines Field - August 17th
Flight Time: five hours.

Whatever really happened, the aircraft was soon fixed, and after more parades and meetings it was on westward the next day! Bob Morgan brought the *Memphis Belle* into land at Mines Field at 4pm, to be met by Governor Earl Warren and other officials. That evening the crew were guests of the 1st Motion Picture Unit at the Warner-Hollywood Theater for the premiere of Irving Berlin's *'This is the Army'*.

Mrs. Morgan No. 3   Mrs. Morgan No. 2

Pilot's Wives

Miss Huckins will succeed Alice Lane Morgan (No. 2) and
Martha Stone Morgan (No. 3) as Mrs. Morgan No. 4. Her
marriage to the romantic pilot is scheduled for Sept. 9.

Patricia Jane Huckins

Enjoying September

Yesterday Jane Francis of East
Lansing, Mich., became the
bride of Capt. Leighton. She's
his schooldays sweetheart.

On Sept. 1 Dinny Kelly Evans
began her honeymoon with
Capt. Evans. They were married
in Walla Walla in July, 1942.

By the time the *Memphis Belle* and crew arrived in Los Angeles, the Press were starting to take a much more critical look at the personalities involved in the Bond Tour - and in particular the somewhat convoluted love-life of one Robert K. Morgan!

Under banner headlines which screamed 'The *Memphis Belle* in Love and War', *Sunday News* journalist Ruth Reynolds put together a somewhat barbed two-page spread that must have taken a considerable amount of work in tracing not only two of Bob Morgan's previous three wives - he went on to marry at least six times - but also Vince Evans' Dinny and Chuck Leighton's sweetheart Jane Francis.

Los Angeles Mines Field to Douglas Long Beach - August 18th
Douglas Long Beach to Los Angeles Mines Field
Flight Time: one hour thirty minutes.

Two flights made this day according to Maintenance Log, from Los Angeles Mines Field to Douglas Long Beach and back again. According to the script, the crew, along with a pilot from Douglas Aircraft arrived for a huge 'meet the workers' event, press conference and additional filming by William Wyler and his crew - footage that was expected to go into the movie.

At the press conference, the media seemed to be more interested in talking about Bob Morgan's love life than the war, the missions and the bond tour. One report shows that when asked about his relationship with Margaret Polk, he tried to explain away the naming of the aircraft by saying that he never was really engaged to Margaret, but that she was only just there when they were breaking champagne over the nose of the Flying Fortress. *'There was a lot of kidding and so we named the ship 'Memphis Belle' after her. Things happen like that and then everyone makes a lot of it. We've known each other a long time and we're good friends - still are for that matter. I never really got involved there. That was just a stunt. I'm in love with Pat - 18 year old Miss Patricia Jane Huckins of San-Antonio, TX - and we're going to be married at the end of the month'.*

After lunch, the crew were to be 'flown back' to Mines Field by a Douglas pilot according to the script but according to Bobs flight records he made two landings that day, so perhaps he was not going to give up his left-hand seat for some company taxi-driver! That evening as guests of Douglas aircraft they dined at the famous Earl Carroll Theatre and Restaurant.

Thursday was to see a civic ceremony and reception at City Hall, Los Angeles, where the crew were greeted on behalf of the state by Governor Earl Warren, Mayor Fletcher Bowron and Sheriff Eugene Biscaluz. In the afternoon the crew over-dubbed their soundtrack for Wyler's movie.

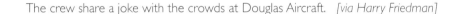

The crew share a joke with the crowds at Douglas Aircraft. *[via Harry Friedman]*

95

<u>TUESDAY</u> <u>August</u> <u>17th</u> Arrive B-17 at Mines Field, El Segundo, California at 4.00PM.

1. Welcoming Committee at airport. Members will greet flyers on landing:
   H.C. Dunham, Public Relations Douglas Aircraft.(phone AShley 4-2941 Ext 346)
   Captain W. F. Raugust, Industrial Serv. Div. Wash DC. Capt Raugust office/phone FItzroy 5292 Ext 315 - residence Ambassador Hotel - phone DR-7011)

(Responsibility for luggage H.D.Dunham).

2. Send luggage by car to either Hollywood Guild Canteen (Mrs Mandell - phone HOllywood 9749) 1284 N. Crescent Heights Blvd, Hollywood California or Del Mar Club, Santa Monica California. (this question to be decided before 4.00PM 8-17-43 and copies of this script changed accordingly). Car for luggage to be furnish by Douglas. Luggage to be tagged "Bomber Crew". Luggage will be placed in one room at the hotel until crew arrives at quarters.

(Resp-Dunham)

3. Members of crew and immediate party will be driven directly to the hotel in cars provided by Douglas Santa Monica.

4. Crew will arrive at hotel at approximately 6.00PM in time to dress for evening. <u>Plans for dinner are open.</u>

(Responsibility cars & tickets Major Wyler AShley 4-2761 residence - Brighton 0-4154)

5. Members of crew will be guests of 1st Motion Picture Unit at Premiere of 'This is the Army' at Warners-Hollywood, 6433 Hollywood Blvd starting at 8.30PM. Cars furnished by army cars of 1st Motion Picture Unit, Culver City. Following the Premiere the army cars will return the crew to their quarters.

(Responsibility H.D.Dunham).

6. Douglas Aircraft will take all necessary action to see that the plane "Memphis Belle" is placed in a protected place (hangar) and security arrangements made.

<u>WEDNESDAY</u> <u>August</u> <u>18th</u>

(Res.cars.Dunham)

1. 9.00AM Cars furnished by Douglas Aircraft will pick up the crew at their quarters and take them to Mines Field.

Motion Picture resp. Maj Wyler

2. The crew and a Douglas Pilot will leaves Mines Field in the "Memphis Belle" in sufficient time to arrive and circle the field at Douglas at exactly 11.00AM. The landing of the plane, the greeting of the workers, the speeches of the crew will all be photographed and used as an actual part of the picture started by Major Wyler in England.

(Resp-Dunham)

2A A guard will be placed on the plane to stop anyone from entering. All restricted material (instrument panel etc) will be covered to prevent it being seen from anyone on the outside of the plane. The workers will be allowed to look at but not touch the plane.

3. Members of Press and Radio present:
   (1)   Los Angeles Times
           Bill Henry, Radio Commentator & Columnist
           Marvin Miles, Aviation Editor
           George Lacks, Photographer

Responsibility Publicity - H. D. Dunham.

   (2)   Los Angeles Examiner
           Sid Hughes
           Ervin Forbes, Photographer
   (3)   Los Angeles Daily News

```
┌──────────────────────────────────────────────────────────────────────────────┐
│ (Note: these              Bill Garrison                                        │
│ names are                 Fred Coffey, Photographer                            │
│ subject to        (4)     Hollywood Citizen-News                               │
│ such revision             John Watts, Reporter-Photographer                    │
│ as Mr. Dunham     (5)     Los Angeles Herald-Express                           │
│ finds necessary)          Don Ryan                                             │
│                           Edward Phillips, Photographer                        │
│                   (6)     Glendale News-Press                                  │
│                           Thomas Welles, Reporter-Photographer                 │
│                   (7)     Wall Street Journal                                  │
│                           Maxwell Thayer, Aviation Editor                      │
│                   (8)     Acme news Pictures                                   │
│                           Stanley Troutman, Photographer                       │
│                   (9)     Burbank Review                                       │
│                           Miss Evaleen Locke, Managing Editor                  │
│                   (10)    World Wide Photo's Inc                               │
│                           Robert Bell, Photographer                            │
│                                                                                │
│               4.  Industrial Services Division, Captain W. F. Raugust, Wash DC │
│                                                                                │
│ (Resp-Dunham) 5.  Press Conference, pictures and interviews from 11:30 to 12:00.│
│                                                                                │
│ (Resp-Dunham) 6.  The crew members will be guests at lunch at Douglas Long Beach.│
│                                                                                │
│ (Resp-Dunham) 7.  After luncheon the crew will be flown back to Mines Field by │
│                   Douglas pilot. Arriving at Mines Field, the crew will be driven│
│                   to their quarters by Douglas Aircraft cars. Security precautions│
│                   will again be taken in protection of the plane "Memphis Belle".│
│                                                                                │
│ (Resp-Dunham) 8.  Members of the crew will be dinner guests of Douglas Aircraft at│
│                   Earl Carroll's Restaurant. The crew will be there at 8:45pm. │
│                   Earl Carroll's is located at 6230 Sunset Blvd, Hollywood (phone│
│                   HOllywood 7101).                                             │
│                                                                                │
│ THURSDAY August 19th                                                           │
│               1.  Civic ceremony and reception at City Hall in Los Angeles.    │
│                   (morning) details in process of being arranged.              │
│                                                                                │
│ (contact      2.  (afternoon) Major Wyler and staff and Captain Raugust will   │
│ Paul Saxson       visit Vega Aircraft, Burbank California for the purpose of    │
│ STanley 7-1241    making arrangements for the plant rally to be held at Vega   │
│ Ext 1616)          Friday during the lunch hour.                               │
│                                                                                │
│               3.  (afternoon) Members of crew will be taken on a tour through a │
│                   movie studio with lunch at the commissary.                   │
│                                                                                │
│               4.  (evening) Entertainment for evening in process of being arranged.│
│                                                                                │
│ FRIDAY August 20th                                                             │
│               1.  Rally at Vega Aircraft during workers lunch hour, program    │
│                   similar to that held at Douglas Aircraft.                    │
│                   Tentative arrangements are in the process for a national radio│
│                   hook-up featuring the members of the crew on Wednesday August│
│                   25th providing War Department approval is received for the crew│
│                   to remain in Los Angeles through Wednesday. The broadcast will│
│                   be made from Santa Ana (contact Captain L. . Steele, Santa Ana│
│                   7043). The crew will be needed from 10:00AM to 8:00pm Wed Aug│
│                   25th for the purposes of rehearsals etc.                     │
└──────────────────────────────────────────────────────────────────────────────┘
```

Two pages of the 'script' for the crew's visit to Los Angeles shows just how large scale and detailed the visit was!

The next day it was to the Vega Aircraft Corporation, which was a subsidiary of the Lockheed Aircraft Company responsible for much of its parent company's production in World War Two. Vega entered a partnership between three companies (Boeing, Vega, and Douglas; abbreviated BVD) to produce the B-17 Flying Fortress. Of over 12,000 B-17s produced by war's end, 2,750 were built by Vega. The company also built two experimental B-17 variants, the XB-38 and the YB-40.

This morning it would be a repeat of the flight out to Douglas but this time flying out to Burbank to meet the workers at Vega. Morgan's flight records for this day show just one landing, so perhaps he did have a taxi driver here!

There were to be two more local flights each under an hour, then on to Dayton OH. It's around this time that the recording gets unclear. It's known they went from Dayton to Camden NC, then to New York.   The whole New York City finalé to the Bond Tour seems to be shrouded in mystery - if only for the fact there is absolutely no contemporary record of it! Yet Morgan describes it all in such great detail. *'...We flew up to New York and landed at Mitchell Field. They put us up in the Waldorf-Astoria for three days. We had another round of parties'.*

Finally, on August 31st they flew the aircraft down to Bolling Field, Washington. Morgan removed the picture of Margaret from the roof panel then he and the crew walked away, dispersed to the four winds.

Bob Morgan brings the *Memphis Belle* in low and fast for the crowds at Douglas Long Beach *(via Harry Friedman)*

Despite the warning contained in the preparation script of 'workers will be allowed to look at but not touch the the aircraft' crowds of workers came out to see the aircraft and crew at Long Beach, where many more autographs and graffiti were added to an already well-marked airframe!

The movie cameras were in evidence again when these pictures were taken, supposedly at Santa Monica. Wyler was known to have been filming at least part of the Bond Tour for inclusion in his 1943 movie. All such scenes ended up on the cutting room floor.

The mission list and names of the ground crew remained in place on the vertical fin throughout the tour for all to see.

THE 1943 WILLIAM WYLER MOVIE

President Roosevelt and his Chief of Staff, General George Marshall, were keen that the American public should be educated as to why they were fighting. Wyler was keen to film the real war and create a documentary. He ran into an old friend, Sy Bartlett. Bartlett had been born Sacha Baraniev in the Ukraine, immigrated to the United States as a child and adopted the name. He had worked as a newspaper reporter before moving to Hollywood to become a screenwriter, then joined the U.S. Army as a captain and was assigned to the Army Pictorial Service. He was not interested in making training films however, and used connections to meet Beirne Lay, Jr., who was on the staff of Army Air Forces General Ira Eaker. Lay had a background in both journalism and Hollywood and arranged for Bartlett to meet General Carl Spaatz, after which Bartlett became Spaatz's aide-de-camp. In mid-June 1942 Bartlett invited Wyler to a reception held at the General's home the day before Spaatz went to

England to set up the Eighth Air Force. At one point in the reception Spaatz stood alone with his Chief of Staff, General Claude E. Duncan. Wyler seized the chance and prodded Bartlett into introducing him to their host. With a boldness characteristic of Hollywood, Wyler referred to Spaatz's secret mission. *"General, I don't know where you're going and I don't know what for, but whatever it is, I think it should be on film."* Wyler went on to explain what films could and should do for the war effort. Spaatz turned to his Chief of Staff and told him to *"Take care of him."* *"Come out to Bolling Field, the day after tomorrow,"* Duncan is supposed to have said. The seeds had been sown.

When Wyler arrived at Bolling Field, Duncan filled out the induction papers. At the heading 'rank' he stopped and looked up thoughtfully. *'Rank... er... would you like to be a Major?'* Wyler thought he was joking, but said *'yes'*. Less than an hour later he was a Major serving in the USAAF! Wyler later recalled *'I put on this uniform that didn't fit and walked down the street with my cigarette, my briefcase and here comes a General. What do I do? Swallow the cigarette? Throw the briefcase away? I threw away the cigarette and saluted. The General saw me and laughed!'*

Legend has it that Major Wyler's orders were clear: get a film crew, proceed to England and make a documentary about the Eighth Air Force. First he went to Hollywood and the FMPU to recruit a crew, get equipment and make arrangements for film developing and editing. He decided to shoot the film in colour - using 'Kodakchrome' filmstock - and 'hired' RKO cameraman William H 'Ace' Clothier and RKO soundman Harold Tannenbaum and William Skall. His writer was Jerry Chodorov.

William Wyler at work! During the winter of 1942/3 Wyler and his crew shot a considerable amount of colour footage at Bassingbourn and Chelveston. Here 91st BG 41-24480 *The Bad Penny* from the 324th BS has been fitted with what suspiciously looks like a pair of 35 mm Mitchell NC cameras in both the waist and radio room hatch positions. The aircraft also is reputed to have carried cameras in the nose and tail. The picture is thought to have been taken on February 1st 1943 when *The Bad Penny* was flown locally for air photography.

The film we know today as 'Memphis Belle' is in fact the fourth attempt Wyler made. In Wyler's files there are two film outlines; one called 'Rendez-VoUS' that was to be a joint US/RAF film story. The second is a draft script from Beirne Lay's 8th Air Force Film Unit dated October 11th 1942 that was revised November 23rd 1942. titled 'Phyllis was a Fortress'. This, we have discovered, is linked to an article published a few days later after the the date of the draft script - on Monday, Oct. 19, 1942 - by TIME Magazine called 'Phyllis the Fortress'. The article detailed a USAAF raid some time earlier on the Potez aircraft factory in Meaulte, France when some 30 German fighter aircraft had fiercely attacked this B-17, forcing the pilot, Charles Paine to belly-land it at an airfield in England.

The draft script and subsequent TIME article were both subject to wartime censorship, but it has been possible to discover that the events identified as to a raid that took place on October 2nd. One participant was the 301st BG, who had 41-24397 named Phyllis assigned to the 352nd BS, 301st BG at Chelveston. On this day the aircraft crash-landed at RAF Gatwick - now London Gatwick Airport - while being flown by Lt Charles Paine Jnr, where the nose had to be cut off to release a crewman. 16 cannon shell and over 200 bullet holes were later counted in the aircraft.

Wyler decided to base himself at one airfield - and he made no secret of why he chose Bassingbourn: 'I picked the base because of its nice comfortable quarters'. Colonel Wray also welcomed the film unit onto 'his' base. Initially the raids were against targets like the submarine pens at St Nazaire and Lorient in occupied France. The Eighth Air Force loss rate had not yet reached unacceptable levels and, by New Year's Eve 1942, Wyler and his camera crew were still alive and celebrated the fact at Claridge's!

William 'Ace' Clothier did much of the filming at Bassingbourn for Wyler. It seems that in postwar interviews Wyler always gave Colonel Stanley Wray the credit for selecting the Memphis Belle, but William Clothier remembered it differently. 'When we first started going on missions and shooting film we had chosen an aircraft called 'Invasion 2nd' piloted by Lt Oscar O'Neil. 'Invasion II' got shot down on one of her missions. We had shot thousands of feet around that plane and suddenly the plane was gone'

42-5070 Invasion II (sometimes recorded as Invasion 2nd) of the 401st BS crashed at Nikolausdorf, Germany with the Lt Oscar O'Neil crew aboard - all were taken PoW. This does however, provide dating evidence in that it shows that up until April 17th, the movie was to feature Invasion II. A few days later Wyler and Clothier decided to look for another aircraft to use. Clothier picks up the story: 'We got in a Jeep and started driving around the base, going from one plane to another, looking them over. All at once there was this perky Petty bathing suit girl staring us in the face and the romantic name, Memphis Belle. Willi pointed his finger at the name and said 'that's it!''

Wyler shot 19 hours of 16 millimetre filmstock, then flew back to the USA to edit the film. Wyler flew back to Hollywood to edit the film. There are previously published indications that Wyler had told Eaker that he would need 90 days to do the job but, for various technical reasons, it could not be completed on time. Wyler cabled Eaker asking for an extra 60 days. The terse reply came: 'Come back or send replacement'. Again, legend has it that Wyler flew back to England to explain in person the difficulties he was having and the need for narration and a music score to be written. Eaker is supposed to granted the him the extra time and Wyler flew back to the States. I

Eventually Eaker allowed Wyler back to the USA. 'The Theater Commander has authorized me to return Major William Wyler, Photographic Section, Eighth Air Force, to the United States on temporary duty to complete a project in which I am very much interested because of its potential value to this Air Force and to the Army Air Forces. Major Wyler is bringing with him approximately 10,000 feet of Kodachrome 16 mm film, most of which he shot personally, depicting our combat missions and activities on the ground'.

SECRET

HEADQUARTERS
EIGHTH AIR FORCE
ETOUSA

4 November 1942.

SUBJECT: Film Unit.

TO   :   Assistant Chief of Staff, A.2.

1. Among the Film Unit's plans for future production is a film based on the experiences of Lieut. Charles Paine and crew of B17F ("Phyllis") on the bombing mission to the Potez factory in Meaulte, Occupied France, on 3 October 1942. The scenario for such a film is now in preparation and when in satisfactory form will be submitted to the Command for approval. Actual production can begin as soon as adequate equipment and personnel become available.

2. The services of the original members of the crew are indispensable to the authenticity and effectiveness of this film.

3. This crew has been transferred to the XIIth Air Force, and the Film Unit requests that the below-named officers and enlisted men be kept in this theatre of operation until the proposed film has been approved and completed.

        Lieutenant CHARLES J. PAINE
        Lieutenant R.H. LONG
        Lieutenant S.A. KOMAREK
        Lieutenant JOHN A. THOMSON
        T/Sgt. BEN P. TAUCHER
        T/Sgt. RALPH SHEETER
        T/Sgt. ARTHUR BOUTHELLIER
        T/Sgt. WALTER PURCELLES
        Sergeant HERBERT PETERSON

WILLIAM WYLER,
Major, A.A.F.,
Film Unit.

What might have been!

The letter from William Wyler to Assistant Chief of Staff requesting that the crew of 41-24397 be held back in the ETO to make a movie. Somehow *Phyllis was a Fortess* does not have the same 'ring' as *Memphis Belle*!

Above right: The title frame of the movie with (left) its Hollywood director William Wyler on the set of one of his movies.

One of the reasons for Wyler needing the extra time was that the filmstock had been damaged while in England. Joseph Josephson of New York was a film technician who worked on the film in London and remembers Wyler almost ruining the movie before it was even shown to the public once: '*Wyler was used to working with professional-grade 35 mm film, but we had to use 16 mm non-professional grade film. You had to make a negative. Wyler didn't know that. He started screening some of the original film after developing. He almost ruined it. He ended up with a lot of scratches. It would have made the film unusable. Willi came to me and asked what he could do as the scenes could not be re-shot. I viewed the film on a viewer to determine the damage, and then explained to him that all the scratches on the celluloid side of the film could be removed by a special process and those on the emulsion side could be removed if they were not too deep. As he was about to return to the USA, I told him that when he arrived in New York he should contact a Mr Friedman at the Deluxe Laboratory on West 55th Street. He had the exclusive rights to a scratch removal process in the USA at the time and this saved the Memphis Belle from disaster*'.

Progress was being made at an ever-increasing pace - on July 19th Wyler's office in Culver City received notification from a Captain Richard G. Elliott of the Air Forces Group, Bureau of Public Relations, War Department that orders had been issued that day for the *Memphis Belle* and crew to spend five days in Los Angeles so as he could complete filming. Captain Elliott confirmed that they would be leaving Columbus, Ohio on August 15th for LA and would be departing for the east during the early morning of August 23rd and enquired if Wyler still intended to cover the leg at Asheville NC, or did the Las Vegas stop fulfil all his requirements?

Then, on July 27th Wyler sent a cable to Colonel R H Magee of the Technical Services Division in the Pentagon. Wyler was resisting Eaker's demand to return to England: *Received orders immediate return before completion of mission stop Staff of writers and cutters working as fast as possible but my presence and supervision essential to editing and accurate effective presentation of film stop Possibilities of this project far greater than previously anticipated and of greater and more immediate benefit that RAF-AAF feature due to complete authenticity and fact that Morgan and crew of Memphis Belle have become national heroes stop Expect finished film will run four or five reels stop Was granted request for Memphis Belle and crew to be sent here on DS for recording of commentary and photography in sound and color of spectacular civic and military reception and their message to war workers for end of picture stop Title and basic idea will be quote the twenty sixth mission unquote built around instructions given to Morgan before returning to the USA by CG 8th AF Stop.*

Clearly Wyler had evolved his thinking from the picture being a two reel color documentary short that had then been 'expanded' into a joint RAF-USAAF project - and the reason was obvious - the *Memphis Belle* and crew were national heroes!

August 26th saw Wyler record in the daily diary of the film; *'Sound tracks of recording made August 22 were heard and best takes selected'*. Clearly progress was being made and things were taking shape - by September 15th, the First Cut had been completed up to the take-off sequence.

A screening of the first cut was arranged for Wednesday September 15th. It was viewed by Major Warren Low, Captain Vince Evans - the *Memphis Belle's* bombardier, who had been retained as a 'technical advisor' once the tour was over - Captain Bill Clothier and Lt Edward B Anhalt.

By early November 1943 Colonel Magee of the Pentagon was again enquiring for a progress update. He telephoned Lt Col A Paul Mantz, Commander of the FMPU, who arranged an urgent meeting between Lt Col William Wyler, Major Ising (animation), Major Van Keuren (production), Captain Baer (production), Lt Anhalt (cutting) and S/Sgt Koenig (writer). As a result of this conference, all decided that it now would be a four-reel film.

Mantz, the former Hollywood stunt pilot, reported that given that the 'Wyler film' had A-1 priority every effort was being made to expedite same. Major Ising stated that he needed another two weeks work to complete the animation, with a further day or two for the ending. There would also be a further two weeks in the Technicolor Lab. S/Sgt Koenig reported that he would have his narration finished in about two weeks but could not finish completely until the final cut was made so that he knew the exact length for timing. It

Six of the many theatre lobby-cards used to promote the movie in various cinemas around the USA.

was expected that the final cut would be complete by around November 25th. The timetable then was for complete cut, exclusive of narration ready by December 2nd. Completion of final cut by December 8th; completion of sound effects cutting by December 13th; completion of first and last two reel musical score by December 22nd; completion of dubbing December 25th. The film would then go to Technicolor where processing would take three to four weeks, being available by mid-January 1944.

With the edited and finished film, Wyler went to Washington for a screening with General Arnold. Legend has it that a further screening was arranged for the President but, on the appointed day the White House cinema was filled with Navy top brass. They insisted the film be shown, although the President had not arrived and Wyler left without meeting Roosevelt. However, a second screening was arranged and, at Roosevelt's request, the two men sat together. The President was very enthusiastic about the film and said it was to be shown everywhere.

However, this is not how FDR's day-to-day diary, kept by members of the White House staff record it. There is a single entry recording Wyler's visit which, for February 15, 1944 shows *'to view army films; Mrs. John Roosevelt, Col. Matherson, Col. Wilson, Lt. Cols. Wyler & Elbert of Army Air Corps.'*

It appears that originally the working title of the film was simply *'The Wyler Film'*. While cutting and editing was taking place at FMPU Culver City the picture was constantly refered to by its 'number' CU-12. This was later changed to *'25 Missions'* to match in with the War Department booklet of the same name written by Ben Grant. However, three days after Wyler's audience with FDR, Francis S. Harmon, Executive Vice

Chairman of the War Activities Committee, Motion Picture Industry, wrote to Secretary of War Henry L Stimson, explaining that arrangements had been made for his Committee to *'...distribute and exhibit the superb Technicolor film made by the Army Air Forces, formerly titled '25 Missions' but now titled 'Memphis Belle'. Five hundred prints in Technicolor portraying this gripping story of a Flying Fortress and its gallant crew are being paid for by our Committee and a special press book is being prepared to bring this picture favorably to the attention of the American people.*

Things now started to move quickly. While the projection copies of the movie were being duplicated, a twelve page booklet *'This is it! The Memphis Belle'* was produced as the core of a Press and Promotions Pack for cinemas and theatres.

This booklet gave an incredible amount of information to Theatre Managers on how to promote the film in their area, and also provides an fascinating insight in to just how far the Air Force were prepared to assist. General Arnold sent a telegraphic 'order' to all Commanding Officers of Army Air Force bases within the USA: *'Motion Picture Memphis Belle made by combat camera crew of Army Air Forces will be exhibited in civilian theatres in near future. There will be no objection to cooperation by installations of your command with local exhibitors providing specifically that no repeat no flights by military aircraft be utilized in this cooperation. Assistance rendered by echelons of your command will be compatible with war-time restrictions and will not repeat not interfere with the military efforts'.*

It seems that the entire Air Force had been placed at the disposal of cinema managers - clearly the Army Air Force wanted to get the film to the attention of as many as possible. This was positive propaganda to the extreme!

The cover was 'flashed' with a quote from 'Boxoffice': *'Every exhibitor who books this film can do so with the conviction that he is providing his patrons with an inspiring, attention-holding, beautifully photographed four reels of drama. In addition he can feel he is helping pay a deserved tribute to America's flying men'.*

The cover of the 1944 *Memphis Belle* Press Book as originally described in the Francis Harmon letter. *(via Harry Friedman)*

The Army Air Force party attending the premiere of William Wyler's movie, seen on the steps of Memphis City Courthouse. Wyler himself is fourth from the right, standing next to Colonel Wray who is fifth.
[USAAF via Harry Freidman]

After keeping the Army Air Force and the public waiting for ten months, at last it was time for an announcement - above the dateline Hollywood Calif March 13, 1944, and the *New York Times* ran a headline that *'Memphis Belle due on April 14'.*

Paramount Pictures agreed to distribute five hundred copies of the movie 'without profit' and screen it in thousands of American cinemas. The Memphis Belle was released on April 15, 1944. Before then though, The War Department and the Air Forces, aptly enough, chose Memphis for the premiere showing of the film on April 5, 1944. After all, the *Memphis Belle* was the star of the show.

Colonel Stanley Wray came to Memphis for the premiere as did Major William E. Clancy, commander of the 324th Squadron. William Wyler came, together with a line-up of veteran bomber pilots. There was a band and Walter P. Chandler, the Mayor of the city of Memphis, officiated at the opening ceremonies. Other government leaders were present.

The real stars of the show though, Bob Morgan and Margaret Polk, for whom the plane had been named, were missing from the list. Memphians did not have to be told why they were not there. The beautiful romance which had sparked the Memphis Belle story was over, the engagement broken. Bob was supposedly away flying, but as for Margaret.... *'My mother saw to it that I had gone to California so I wouldn't be embarrassed by all the publicity. So I was not at the Premiere'.*

Lillard M'Gee of *The Commercial Appeal* in Memphis described the premier under the headline 'Memphis Belle hits as vivid war picture' *"Memphis Belle, the Army's own story of bombing attacks on Axis Germany opened yesterday with a world premier at the Malco and will also be shown at the Lowe's State starting tomorrow.*

The picture is a technicolor production so vivid that one feels that one actually is riding in the 'Memphis Belle' as it makes its 25th and last attack on Germany, dropping its bombs on the submarine base at Wilhelmshaven. Premiere of the picture got under way here yesterday with a group of Army Air Force officers and motion picture men in town for the event.

The distinguished visitors were officially greeted at the City Hall at noon by Mayor Chandler, were entertained at a luncheon at the Peabody by Paramount Pictures and last night were introduced by Mayor Chandler from the Malco stage. Heading the group of visitors was Col. Stanley R Wray, who was group commander over the 'Belle' in England, and appears as the briefing officer in the picture. Lieut. Col. William Wyler, former motion picture producer who edited the picture; Maj. A.A. Schecter of the Army Air Forces Public Relations Office in Washington and Maj. William E Clancy, commander of the squadron in which the "Memphis Belle" flew and pilot of the plane 'Dame Satan' seen in the picture... ...Of the war generally Colonel Wray commented: "We are firmly convinced we're fighting the war in the right way with our long range strategic bombing, striking at the Axis bases of supply. The bombing is going on night and day and I do not believe the German people can absorb it. Civilians often want quick results and fail to understand the purpose of strategic bombing. Strategic bombing means fewer men in the ground forces are going to lose their lives. It means that some day some German soldier is going to reach for another belt of machine gun cartridges and there wont be another one. I feel that under the bombing the Germans will break at home quicker than they will on the front. When that will be, no one can say. One won't be able to tell even five days in advance."

Colonel Wray, in discussing the bombing raids generally, declared that they are a matter of every man and every ship working together. 'I remember,' he said, 'on our first raid over the Channel there were eight ships. Now 1000 go out at a time. When we were there they wanted an all-out raid. Men had to be recalled from leave. Now, they have enough men and enough ships that they can go out in relays, hundreds of planes at a time....

...A group of officers from Dyersburg who were present included Capt. William E Beasley, Capt. James Bullock, Capt. Olin Hubbard, Capt. James Hensley, Capt Leonard Santoro and Lieut. Robert Bercu, all of whom served with Colonel Wray.

Left to right: Colonel Wyler, Colonel Wray and Major Clancy (commanding Officer of the 324th BS) at the Peabody Hotel, Memphis on 6 April 1944 for the Premiere of Colonel Wyler's movie. *[USAAF via Harry Freidman]*

To give an idea of the scale and scope of the film's release, in New York alone the film was shown as part of a double-feature in fourteen Broadway cinemas: the Paramount, Roxy, Astor, Strand, Hollywood, Lowe's, Criterion, Globe, Manhattan Gotham, Palace, Rialto Lowe's State, the Embassy Newsreel and the Trans-Lux Broadway and Forty-Ninth Street.

A few days after the movies release, General 'Hap' Arnold wrote to Barney Balaban, the President of Paramount Pictures: *'I am informed that already definite arrangements have been made with nearly 9,000 theatres in this country for the showing of the film. As you know, I consider it an important piece of documentary history which has caught the spirit of our air and ground personnel in true and memorable fashion. I have been anxious that it be brought home to the largest possible number of our citizens on the home front to assure fullest possible understanding of the problems faced and accomplishments achieved in the fighting theatres. The efforts of your organization are bringing my wish to fulfilment, and I am grateful'.*

The movie made an incredible impact on the psyche of Americans, aided without doubt, by the extremely intensive publicity campaign - queues formed at theatres wherever it was shown. The same thing happened in the United Kingdom when it was released there on October 16th 1944, being distributed, according to the British Film Institute, by MGM. It was reality with the Hollywood touch - it touched a nerve, lodged in the soul somewhere so people simply 'remembered' it.

The Press Book that went ahead of the movie revealed there was level of co-operation afforded to Paramount by the Army Air Force that was just about as high as it could be, considering there was a war on. It is more that likely that the War Department and the President were discreetly preparing the American Public for the high-risk gamble that was to come. It is known that the impact of any movie is at its highest during the first six weeks or so of its release, and given that, the timing was perfect - after all, the message in the movie was clear - 'we're taking punishment, yes. We're learning, and we are dishing it out. We Will Win'. The film provided a patriotic yet revealing insight into the combat and sacrifices that lay ahead for the nation with the gamble that was the then forthcoming but highly secret invasion of Europe in June 1944 - an invasion that led to eventual victory over Nazi tyranny

The inside of Hangar One, at the Spokane Air Depot (SPAD) and a line of B-17Fs slowly have components removed for repair or refurbishment.

After Bob Morgan and the crew walked away from the *Memphis Belle* at Bolling Field, Washington DC, the aircraft languished there for nearly three weeks. Finally a Captain S Strahan left Washington DC on September 21st and flew the aircraft in a series of short hops across the country again to Spokane, Washington State, where it arrived on September 25th according to the Maintenance Log, or the 28th if you read the Spokane newspapers.

Located 12 miles west of the city of Spokane, Washington, the huge Spokane Air Depot sat adjacent to US Highway 2, where construction crews had poured the foundations for the first buildings of the Army Air Depot - later to become Fairchild Air Force Base - on March 2, 1942.

Here the aircraft underwent IRAN - Inspect and Repair As Necessary - in other words a complete overhaul with the intention of returning it to combat operations. By now, though, the Army Air Force was taking delivery of the new more advanced 'G' model B-17s, so 41-24485 would be relegated to become a training aircraft.

PAINT & DOPE SHOP
AIRPLANE STATUS CHART
Sheet No. A
Fuselage Inside

S-494

Type B-17F Serial No. 41-24485 Started 11/4/43 Est. Date Out 11/25/43

Memphis Belle

COCKPIT	Crew Chief	Fore
Fuel Press ⊗ Oil Press ⊗ Oil Temp. ⊗ R.P.M. ⊗ Suction ⊗	Clark	Scheller
Manif. Press ⊗ Cyl. Head Temp. ⊗ Air Speed Ind. ⊗ Hyd. Press. ⊗	Clark	Scheller
Fuel Air Ratio ⊗ Carburetor Temp. N.A De-Icer Gauge ⊗		
Touch-Up Instrument & Misc. Switch Panels ⊗		
Fill in Engraved Letters with Wax as needed ⊗		
Repaint all Emergency Switches and Handles ⊗		
Placard for Fuel ⊗ Placard for Air Speed ⊗		
Control Columns as needed ⊗ Main Control Assy. ⊗		
General Touch-Up and Misc. Lettering & Placards ⊗		
Check for Overspray ⊘		

AREA FROM COCKPIT TO BOMBARDIER'S COMP.

Oxygen Press. Stencil ⊗ British Adapter Stencil ⊗ NA
Comb Controls Stencil ⊗ Emergency Door Stencil ⊗
Voltage Regulator Box Stencil ⊗

BOMBARDIER'S COMPARTMENT

Air Speed Indicator ⊘ Bomb-Bay Door Placard ⊘
Tone & Tape Heater Ducts N/A Panels & Lettering as Needed ⊗
General Touch-Up ⊘ Check for Overspray ⊗

BOMB-BAY COMPARTMENT

Landing Gear Stencil ⊗ Emergency Bomb Release Stencil ⊗
Comb Door Placard ⊗ Guard Rail Stencil ⊗

RADIO COMPARTMENT

Paint Alcohol Tank Cap ⊗ Anti-Icer Stencil ⊗
Remove Tank Stencil ⊗ Rear Door Stencil ⊗
General Touch-Up N/A ⊗ Check for Overspray ⊘

REAR FUSELAGE INSIDE

Deflector Stencils ⊗ Waist Gun Load Stencil ⊗
Emergency Door Stencil ⊗ Dome Light Switch ⊗
Acid Proof Paint Around Toilet ⊗ Fuel Transfer Stencil ⊗
To Open Window Stencils ⊗ Kite & Transmitter Stencil N/A

REAR GUNNER COMPARTMENT

Emergency Door Stencil ⊗ Emergency Pull Red ⊗

MISCELLANEOUS

All above articles signed off on authorized work sheet ⊘
All Paint & Overspray Removed from all Glass ⊗

CODE MARKINGS & ABBREVIATIONS
S----Stencil L----Left R----Right O----Work to be done N.A. Not Applicable
/----In progress X----Finished P.A.----Previously Accomp.

PAINT & DOPE SHOP
AIRPLANE STATUS CHART
Sheet No. B
Outside

S-494

Type B-17F Serial No. 41-24485 Started _____ Est. Date Out _____

EMPENNAGE

Dope, Tape, & Paint Elevators ⊗ Finish Code S. ⊗
De-Icer Boots, painted ⊘ Tested _____ ; Cell Letters ⊗
Do Not Move Gun S. ⊗ Insp. Plates & Control Doors ⊗
Sight Control Access S. ⊗ Paint Rear Gunsight ⊗
Rudder Trim Tab. Plate S. ⊗ General Touch-Up ⊘

FUSELAGE

Fire Ext. S. ⊗ Escape Panel S. ⊗ Insignias, R. ⊗
Turrets as needed ⊘ Life Raft Compartment & Control S. ⊗
Tank Vent S. ⊗ Hyd. Tank Drain & Vent S. ⊗
Model S. ⊗ Serial No. S. ⊗ Crew Weight S. ⊗
Octane S. ⊗ Aromatic Fuel S. ⊗ Exter. Power S. ⊗
Prop. Anti-Icer Tank Drain ⊗ Fuel Trans. Drain S. ⊗
General Touch-Up ⊗ Oil Separator Drain S. ⊗
Paint & Overspray Removed from Windows & Insulators ⊘
Relief Drain S. ⊗

WINGS

Insignias, L. _____ Finish Code S.L. ⊗ NA R. NA Drain Cock S.L. ⊗ R. ⊗
Water Drain S.L. ⊗ R. ⊗ Aileron Tab. & Control S.L. ⊗ R. ⊗
Flap Control S.L. ⊗ R. ⊗ Jack S.L. ⊗ R. ⊗ Moor S.L. ⊗ R. ⊗
Fuel Cell Door Caution S.L. ⊗ R. ⊗ Battery Vent S.L. ⊗ R. ⊗
Vacuum Pump Ex. S.L. ⊗ Booster Pump S. L. ⊗ R. ⊗
Engine Fuel Drain S. L. ⊗ R. ⊗ Feeder Fuel Drain S.L. ⊗ R. ⊗ PA
Supchg. Lub. Tank Drain & Vent S.L. ⊗ R. ⊗
Feeder Tank Filler Overflow S. L. ⊗ R. ⊗
Engine Tank Filler Overflows S. L. ⊗ R. ⊗
Bomb Rack Elect. Connection S. L. ⊗ R. ⊗
Fuel Filler Caps & Gauges S. L. ⊗ R. ⊗
Outside Air Temp. S. L. ⊗ R. ⊗ No Step S. L. ⊗ R. ⊗
Feeder Fuel & Gauge S. L. ⊗ R. ⊗ Aromatic Fuel S. L. ⊗ R. ⊗
Octane S. L. ⊗ R. ⊗ Disc. Elect. Wire S.L. ⊗ R. ⊗ Walkway S. ⊗ R. ⊗
Hoist S. L. ⊗ R. ⊗ Paint Battery Boxes ⊗
De-Icer Boots Painted ⊗ Tested _____ Ailerons, L. ⊗ R. ⊗
Overspray Removed from all Glass & Insulators ⊘

REMARKS

It seems everyone kept material relating to the famous aircraft! Bud Stratford did his share of 'collecting'! True, they are of poor quality, but the worksheets for 41-24485 show some of the work done from the Paint and Dope Shop at Spokane Air Depot. The work on the aircraft was expected to take three weeks.

Clarence E 'Bud' Stratford was a Spokane Air Depot Foreman in the Paint Department who worked on what could be called the 'first restoration' that took place. *'We had a Depot Inspection and Repair line set up between Hangars Three and Four. This was an eleven station line. An airplane would first be routed to what we called 'Flight test and Inspection'. There it would be decided what had to be done to it to put it back in new condition and a worksheet made on it. All secret equipment would be removed and sent to the Bombsight building. From there it would progress to the cleaning stations where it would be thoroughly cleaned inside and out. Then all parts and items that could not be repaired on the airplane were removed and routed to the various repair shops. Those items beyond repair and not in Air Force stock were manufactured. All items would return to designated stations to be re-installed on the airplane. The routing station would tag each item, listing each shop it had to go to and it was the responsibility of these shops to deliver it to the next shop on the tag when they had accomplished and signed off their part of the*

PAINT & DOPE SHOP
AIRPLANE STATUS CHART
SHEET NO. C
Outside Miscellaneous

S-494

Type B-17F Serial No. 41-24485 Started _____ Est. Date Out _____

ENGINE NACELLES & MISCELLANEOUS

Engine Oil S.1 ⊗ 2 ⊗ 3 ⊗ 4 ⊗ Caution S. 2 ⊗ 3 ⊗
Fuel Pump Drain S. 1 ⊗ 2 ⊗ 3 ⊗ 4 ⊗
Starter Pull S. 1 ⊗ 2 ⊗ 3 ⊗ 4 ⊗ Blower Drain S.1 ⊗ 2 ⊗ 3 ⊗ 4 ⊗
Feathering Pump Drain S. 1 ⊗ 2 ⊗ 3 ⊗ 4 ⊗
Oil Heater Receptical S. 1 ⊗ 2 ⊗ 3 ⊗ 4 ⊗
Water Drain S. 1 ⊗ 2 ⊗ 3 ⊗ 4 ⊗ Fuel Support S. 1 ⊗ 2 ⊗ 3 ⊗ 4 ⊗
Supchg. Lub. Tank Vent & Drain S. 1 ⊗ 2 ⊗ 3 ⊗ 4 ⊗
Oil Drain S. 1 ⊗ 2 ⊗ 3 ⊗ 4 ⊗
Access Case Drain S. 2 ⊗ Glycol Pump Drain S. 2 ⊗
Discon. Bonding S. 1 ⊗ 2 ⊗ 3 ⊗ 4 ⊗
Lift Starter Brush S. 1 ⊗ 2 ⊗ 3 ⊗ 4 ⊗
Paint & Stencil Props. 1 ⊗ 2 ⊗ 3 ⊗ 4 ⊗
Cowling as needed 1 ⊗ 2 ⊗ 3 ⊗ 4 ⊗
Cowl Flaps as needed 1 ⊗ 2 ⊗ 3 ⊗ 4 ⊗
All Paint & Overspray Removed from all working surfaces ⊗

DISCREPANCY & FINAL CHECK AFTER RUN UP

1. slippage marks on wheels — Clark Scheller
2. remove paint on all leading edges inc de-icer boots — Wm R Doyle
3. slippage marks on all instruments — Clark Scheller
4. comply with T.O. 01-1-133 — Wm R Scheller
5. stencil & T.O. Hyd Fluid in Struts (on all 4) — Clark Scheller
6. touch up _____
7. apply "no step" stencil in bomb. comp.
8. Paint Gun mounts in rear fuselage — Wm R

CODE MARKINGS & ABBREVIATIONS
S----Stencil L----Left R----Right O----Work to be done
/----In Progress X----Finished PA----Previously Accomp.
N. A. ----Not Applicable

C. E. STRATFORD Gen. Fore.

necessary work. I think the Paint Department was the last on the list and possibly the only one that received 99% of all parts removed from the planes. We had two stations on the line where we would completely repaint the airplane, inside and out, replacing insignia, instruction plates, and nomenclature.

Clearly this meant that the aircraft was pretty much stripped of all removable equipment. Nose installation off, turrets out - almost certainly the pilots seats were removed for ease of access also. From Bud Stratford's description, there is a very good possibility - to the point of certainty - that much, if not all of the equipment used in combat in England was removed and different items put back in to complete the refurbishment! Bud continues describing the process:

One of my crew chiefs was a young commercial artist named Herb Schedin, who often repainted any artwork on the machines we had through. When we had the Memphis Belle through, we were asked to reproduce exactly all the drawings, crew names, bombing missions, lettering etc after the aircraft had been repaired and repainted. This was a cinch for Herb. Unfortunately he was not with us too long - the Technical Orders of the day recommended the use of carbon-tetrachloride as a solvent and cleaning agent on all aircraft and aircraft parts. It was later prohibited when they discovered just how toxic it was, but those orders came too late to save Herb.

There was a section of skin on the left wing where a 20 mm shell had gone through and had had a piece of

Above: An AAF officer talks to an Air Depot worker in front of the *Memphis Belle*.

How the arrival of the *Memphis Belle* was reported in the Spokane Air Depot newspaper 'Wings'.

"MEMPHIS BELLE"—Buxom heroine of 25 missions over Nazi Europe is undergoing a thorough overhaul at SPAD for return to enemy skies and new adventures. "Keep 'Em Flying" repair crews will put the battle-scarred Amazon into shape for her return to battle.

Workers in the Paint Shop at Spokane Air Depot re-finish parts of B-17F's during the time the Memphis Belle was undergoing overhaul there.

fabric doped over it. This 'hole' interested me, so I got a pair of snips, and cut a square piece out - with the 'hole' still in it - took it in the shop and had the fellows paint a reproduction of the nose of the Belle with all the information on it'.

When Bob Morgan completed his 25th officially credited mission he wrote to tell Margaret Polk that he would paint out the name and that perky Petty Girl before handing the aircraft over to another pilot and crew. When they returned to the USA for the Bond Tour they kept the name and artwork in place - it was still there when they walked away from the aircraft at Bolling Field. Morgan's romance with Margaret may have ended, but the aircraft and name was now famous all over the USA, and perhaps someone within the Air Force thought that the name, markings and mission list might just mean something to the students who might fly in it. It might just make them proud to be flying and training on such a famous aircraft.

The overhaul lasted until November 30th 1943, when Captain W L Bollinger took 41-24485 up for a one hour test flight. Then, on December 1st, Lt Col R T Bankard took it up for a further 1 hour 20 minute flight after which he complained the gyroscope was sluggish and the heaters were inoperative!

Things then settled down to the daily grind of flying training in the sunshine when the aircraft was transferred to 815th Bomb Squadron, part of the Third Bomber Command at MacDill Field, Florida, located eight miles south of downtown Tampa. Originally known as Southeast Air Base, Tampa, it was later named MacDill Field in honor of Colonel Leslie MacDill.

Over the years many Air Force personnel have contacted us regarding their memories of flying training on the aircraft. Many of their memories are broadly similar, but that in itself demonstrates the repetitiveness of flying training - we cannot vouch for the accuracy of what they recall, for very little primary source documentation has been located from these times - all we do can is to pay tribute to 'those who also served' and to say 'they were there'!

Howard W. Koepke from Pittsburgh, Pennsylvania: *'I flew the Memphis Belle at McDill Field, Tampa, Florida. The time was March - May 1944. This was crew training following Transition. She was a little 'run down' at the time but everyone wanted to fly her'.*

Former T/Sgt John L Knight wrote us back in 1982, following an article in *Sergeants* magazine: *I head read and heard about the famous aircraft and its crew but we were unaware that the aircraft was at McDill Field until our crew were dispatched out to the ship itself and saw the names and pictures on the fuselage. We couldn't believe it and it was the best-equipped and smoothest-flying plane we flew in during our three months training at McDill. We were specially impressed by the sheepskin that someone had installed in the ball turret seat. Our ball turret gunner was especially pleased for it transformed a very cold spot into a much warmer one in flight!*

George W Bachmann Jnr from Akron, Ohio: *In March or April 1944 our crew flew a training flight in her. It was a good flight, and a whole lot quieter than any other other planes I flew in afterwards. That was the only plane that had any type of covering on the inside. I was only eighteen when I flew in the Memphis Belle. From Tampa, Florida I went to England in June of 1944, landed in England, the first of July, which was my nineteenth birthday. I went on to finish 35 missions with the 367th Bomb Squadron, 306th Bomb Group as a Waist Gunner'.*

Eugene Gerbitz was a waist gunner with the 452nd BG: *I flew in the Memphis Belle from MacDill during August/September 1944. At that time the plane was housed in a hangar and was only used as an extra plane when others were in for servicing. I was on a very short flight on her - lasting about ten minutes - as an engine caught fire and we had to make a forced landing.*

Navigator Harry Dodson: *Our crew flew in it two or three times. What I remember most about the Memphis Belle was that the navigator's desk and work area were in front of the co-pilot and was the only one I ever saw that way.*

Paul Martin from Chatham, Massachusetts: *I first met the Belle after her war bond drive at MacDill Field in Tampa where she was assigned the job of training new combat crews. I'm living proof she did a great job when I completed my last mission on December 24th 1944. I vividly recall the feeling I had when I learned the Belle had been assigned to me for a practice bombing mission. I also recall the problem we had getting her off the ground when she suddenly lost considerable power as we passed that point of no return! There was a moment when I thought we would uphold the legend of 'one-a-day-in-Tampa-Bay' but we finally coaxed her off the ground.*

Paul H Martin in front of the *Memphis Belle* at MacDill, Florida. As can be seen, the aircraft was used as a 'backdrop' for many souvenir photographs!

T/Sgt Red Haney (left) and S/Sgt George W 'Ruff House' Bachman Jnr in front of the *Memphis Belle* at MacDill, Florida.

Joe Pearce, Milford, Delaware: *I was honored to pilot the Memphis Belle on a training flight at MacDill Field, Tampa, FL in the spring of 1944. I can still remember the thrill of climbing into the cockpit of that famous aircraft'.*

It seems that the AAF were not beyond using the 'fame' of the *Memphis Belle* as a training aid, as Lt Col Frank Holan explains: *Late in 1943 and early in 1944 I was assigned to the gunnery school at Yuma, Arizona, as an Aerial Gunnery Instructor. The purpose of the school was to turn out gunners skilled in the so-called 'flexible' use of air- cooled .50-caliber machine guns--fighter pilots were trained in 'fixed' gunnery, meaning that they had to aim the whole aircraft at the enemy, while people trained in 'flexible' gunnery used guns that could be moved in elevation and traverse while the aircraft they were in moved on a more or less steady course. While I was at Yuma, the then current crew of the Memphis Belle visited the base to give the class, most of whom would eventually wind up as bomber crew members, the benefit of their combat experience.*

The briefing consisted of two parts: descriptions of combat missions (assignment of German fighter units to defense areas; "smart" versus "dumb" fighter pilots; the most difficult maneuver to cope with — fighters circle at 12:00 o'clock high, hit formation, and flash past your nose upside down) followed by a question-and answer period.

Robert M 'Bob' Hosan of Wilmington, Delaware: '*I received gunnery training at Tyndall Field in Florida. It was there I flew aboard the Memphis Belle, I am certain I flew in it on at least one training mission - I can even remember the name of the pilot, a Lt Ludwig who hailed from my home state of Pennsylvania. I distinctly being 'in awe' at being able to fly this famous aircraft. At the age of 18 these things really cast a spell on a young, aspiring flyer'.*

William Wintersteen from Danville, Pennsylvania; '*I was sent to MacDill in September 1944, and flew the Memphis Belle a number of times. The Belle was a horror to fly! The throttles were all mis-aligned with the others - it would've been impossible to fly formation. The supercharger levers were likewise all out of line. Oil was splattered over the nacelles and wings. In spite of all this I was proud - VERY proud to have flown the Queen!'*

Jack Novey, San Francisco CA: '*I was an instructor gunner at MacDill Field and was thrilled to fly the Memphis Belle many times training gunners - all the combat vets wanted to fly in her. We took her over from Florida to Cuba for Presidente Fulgencio Batista's 4th July celebrations and for a picnic! At the time she was fitted with camera mounts on all the guns to allow us to check students accuracy'.*

George L Edgar of Cincinnati, OH: '*I had the honor of flying in the Belle while in training at MacDill, Florida in June 1944. As most of our training was in G-Model 17s it was quite an experience to get into the Memphis Belle and look her over completely. Our particular training mission on this afternoon did not include any specific duties for me as Bombardier, so I just sat up there in the 'spacious' nose in the padded armchair taking in the scenery. When our mission that afternoon was over we spent a long time looking over the ship, commenting on the duty she had seen and trying to anticipate what our combat*

Frank E Ring of McKeesport PA was assigned to 376th BG at MacDill and provides this picture showing the 'J4' markings

tour would be like. I became Lead Bombardier of the 835th Bomb Squadron, 486th Bomb Group at Sudbury in England. On another occasion I flew the Belle on a five hour twelve plane combat formation flight with full crew. We were told at briefing that there would be times on combat where after five hours we would just be turning around for another five hour trip back to base! I tried to imagine what it must have been like to have been in the Belle on one of her raids but my imagination left out many things that I was soon to experience'.

Davis M Gammage of Birmingham, Alabama: 'I flew the Memphis Belle first on April 18th 1945. It was a high altitude 'max effort' formation of over 50 B-17s with a bomb drop and simulated attacks by P-51 fighters. My navigator Robert A Cook was from Memphis and was so excited getting to navigate the famous plane named after a girl from his home town. The mission went pretty smoothly except from several 'war weary' features. Cook missed part of his navigation problem due to either missing or faulty equipment. From the pilot's standpoint she was sluggish on the controls - the turbos must have been badly worn; the engines were slow to respond on demand for power and when I pulled the throttles back to ease off the power the response was slow, so we kept trying to either catch-up or stop flying through the formation. I remember there were numerous 'holes' in the airframe that had been metalled and rivetted over, particularly in the radio room area. When Bob Cook came out of the rear side door after the mission he was beating on the side of the plane - then he walked up to the right main landing gear and kicked the wheel. He used a good bit of profanity describing his hurt foot and his disappointment of his lousy navigation problem. We flew her several times after that, but I don't remember dates and times.

Dr Arthur L Ennis of Gadsden, AL was a waist gunner with the 91st BG at Bury St Edmunds on B-17s. 'I think I flew in it [the Memphis Belle] to Mitchell Field in 1944. I got up in to the upper turret during the flight, although we were socked in by the weather. We were flying along when all of a sudden the plane took a violet dip and turn and the pilot said he throught he had seen the shadow of another aircraft and so took evasive action. I dont remember if I got into the tail or ball turret. Visibility in the waist was limited, so I probably walked around a lot. On the way back we had electrical problems. [Most of] the crew were sacked out in the radio room and we were awakened by one crewmember thrashing around. One had his O2 [oxygen supply] come loose. We plugged him back in and he did ok'.

Charlotte Kates of Cincinnati, Ohio contacted us back in 1992 - she remembered working on the aircraft at Sebring: 'The Memphis Belle had hairline cracks from metal stress. We drilled holes at the end of each and then patched two-and-a-half-times the size of the crack. There was also corroded aluminium around the tailwheel where the tail-gunner sat, it was all badly corroded, for it had been used as a urinal. It was up to us women to remove the old metal and replace it with new. Due to almost total blindness and emphysema, I've been hospitalised for two years - and have asked my friend Edna Plunkett to help with this letter. I blame the carbon-tetrachloride, asbestos and chrome paint for my lung condition to date - although it's fifty years later!'

Lt Col. Robert S 'Bob' Wardner of St Petersburg, Florida; Enclosed is a copy [opposite] of my Clearance to fly the Memphis Belle from Hendricks Field, Sebring, Florida on May 20th 1945. Hendricks was B-17 Transition School. My brief temporary tour of duty there was to instruct B-17 pilots how to ditch a B-17 by demonstrating it to them in a PBY OA-10 out in the Gulf of Mexico. I was also a B-17 Instructor pilot so when I spotted the Memphis Belle on the flightline, I was able to fly it that weekend for pure enjoyment of being able to say I flew that beautiful and historic bird. She was without armament, not entirely clean, but mechanically in excellent condition. It was a highlight in my B-17 flying experience.

ARMY AIR FORCES
AIRCRAFT ARRIVAL REPORT

A	OPERATIONS OFFICE	POST OPERATIONS			DATE
	ADDRESS	HENDRICKS FIELD, SEBRING, FLORIDA			5-20-45

B	PILOT'S NAME	RANK	HOME STATION	ORGANIZATION	AIRCRAFT NUMBER
	WARDNER R.S.	2D LT	HENDRICKS	EFTC	41-24485

NAME, INITIALS, RANK, HOME STATION OF OTHER OCCUPANTS

"MEMPHIS BELLE"

CAUTHEN, R.H. 2D LT DEI
DUNNE, T. SGT "
CHIAPPINI, C.W. SGT "
BARRIS, R.G. SGT "

AVON PK
4-18-45
Robt S. Wardner

LIST ADDITIONAL PASSENGERS ON SEPARATE SHEET

C	WEATHER DATA	EXISTING LOCAL	O 86/56 W6	ALTIMETER SETTINGS
	EXISTING ROUTE	WZ35 O	MM 40 O	LOCAL 2998 E

DESTINATION (LATEST)	as shown	TIME	DESTINATION
ALTERNATE (LATEST)		TIME	ALTERNATE

FORECASTS (ESTIMATED FLIGHT TIME PLUS 2 HOURS)

RESET ALTIMETER BEFORE APPROACH

ROUTE: Clear to 3/10 W near 4000', usby 7-10 min, slight turb to 3000'

DESTINATION: Clear, usby 8-10 min of wind 60° 8-10 mph

ALTERNATE:

WINDS ALOFT GIVE ALT. DIR. VEL. AS PILOT REQUESTS: 2000' 100° 10-12 mph

AAF FORM 23A REQUIRED ☐	NOT REQUIRED ☐	FORECASTER Capt K Diltrel	TIME 1350 E

D	FLIGHT PLAN	(PILOT COMPLETES) RADIO CALLS	448	TYPE OF AIRCRAFT B-17	PILOT (LAST NAME ONLY) WARDNER	POINT OF DEPARTURE SEBRING, FLORIDA

| 1 | ☑ CFR ☐ IFR | ALT CFR ROUTE DIRECT TO WEST PALM | 2 | ☑ CFR ☐ IFR | ALT CFR ROUTE AIRWAYS TO MIAMI | 3 | ☑ CFR ☐ IFR | ALT CFR ROUTE AIRWAYS TO WEST PALM | 4 | ☑ CFR ☐ IFR | ALT CFR ROUTE DIRECT TO HENDRICKS |

AIRPORT OF FIRST INTENDED LANDING HENDRICKS FLD	TRUE AIR SPEED 160	TRANSMITTING FREQUENCIES 4495 KC 6710 KC KC	RECEIVER ONLY ☐ NO RADIO ☐

PROPOSED TAKE-OFF TIME 1415	EST. TIME ENROUTE 3:00 to	ALTERNATE AIRPORT	HOURS OF FUEL (CRUISING) 8-00	INSTRUMENT RATING NONE ☐ TYPE W	FLIGHT PRIORITY 3-Y

REMARKS: SHOW FIXES WHICH WILL BE REPORTED WHILE ON INSTRUMENT FLIGHT.

ROUND ROBIN FLIGHT PLAN

PILOT'S SIGNATURE: Robert S. Wardner

TOWER FREQUENCIES DESTINATION 718 KC	ALTERNATE KC	WEATHER CODE RECEIVED ☐ YES ☑ NO	TO DESTINATION	MILEAGE DEST. TO ALTERNATE 3Y0	☐ COMMAND PILOT ☐ SENIOR PILOT ☐ CONTRACT PILOT OF CARGO AIRCRAFT ☑ PILOT

E		FLIGHT CLEARANCE AUTHORIZATION	

SUBMITTED TO	TIME	BY	W. H. Hissing COL	OPERATIONS IDENTIFICATION NO.
TIME APPROVAL RECEIVED	CONTROL INSTRUCTIONS RECEIVED		CLEARING AUTHORITY B. F. Ke...	Fd W AC
INSTRUCTIONS AND APPROVAL TRANSMITTED TO PILOT OR TOWER BY:	ACTUAL TAKE-OFF TIME		CLEARANCE OFFICER	HR

G	THIS COPY TO BE GIVEN TO PILOT.	ARRIVAL REPORT	Pilot will complete "Arrival Report" and present to line crewman meeting the arriving aircraft, for his information. Line crewman will then forward to the operations office. Home station will be notified in the event of an overnight stop.

DATE AND TIME OF ARRIVAL	R.O.N. ☐ YES ☐ NO	SERVICE REQUIRED ☐ GAS ☐ OIL	DESIRED DATE AND TIME OF DEPARTURE	DEPARTING FOR:
WHERE PILOT CAN BE REACHED AT THIS STATION	REMARKS			LINE CREWMANS SIGNATURE

OUT TO GRASS LEADS TO A SECOND HOMECOMING!

The Germans surrendered on May 8th 1945, although the war in the Pacific would grind on until August 14th, the United States Army Air Force found itself with a surplus of unwanted B-17s, for during the closing months the brunt of the bombing campaign was being conducted using B-29s. No matter how glorious its past, the Air Force no longer needed the battered and worn-out B-17 called the *Memphis Belle*. On July 2nd 1945 it was flown to Altus, Oklahoma by an unknown pilot.

Altus was one of a number of 'gathering places' for unwanted aircraft. Here 41-24485 was placed on storage status on September 9th and then on October 18th 1945 passed to the Reconstruction Finance Corporation (RFC), the government agency tasked with the disposal of surplus military equipment.

RECONSTRUCTION FINANCE CORPORATION
Office of Surplus Property—Aircraft Division—Educational Disposal Section
WASHINGTON 25, D. C.

PURCHASE ORDER

Agreement No.

Order No.

Date....March 30,.............19..46.

Ship to:.. City of Memphis
Full Name of Institution

Courthouse, Memphis, Tennessee.
No.   Street   City   State   Signature

Catalog No.	Quantity	Nomenclature	Type	Disposal Cost		Quantity Shipped	Date Shipped
				Unit	Total		
RFC No. 84	1	Airplane, Serial No. 41-24485, known as "Memphis Belle"	B-17	$350.00	350.00		

For instruction, education, and memorial purposes.

Above: with the Reconstruction Finance Corporation's catalog number '84' crudely marked on the nose - barely visible in this picture just under the Petty Girl's feet - the *Memphis Belle* awaits the wreckers.

Left: the Purchase Order authorising the sale of 'Airplane Serial No. 41-24485 known as 'Memphis Belle' to the city of the same name.

Below: The *Memphis Belle* seems to have been parked in a special area at Altus, here seen alongside the famous and much-autographed B-24 Liberator *'Five Grand'*. [all via Harry Friedman]

It seemed that the *Memphis Belle* was about to be scrapped. With the outbreak of peace in 1945, the Army Air Force no longer wanted the aircraft, and so it was flown to Altus for storage and eventual scrapping. Mayor Chandler allowed no time to be wasted, once the war was over. On August 25, just eleven days after the end of the war in the Pacific, Chandler made his next move to obtain the aircraft for Memphis. While the *Memphis Belle* and her fame were fresh in everyone's mind, Chandler petitioned the War Department once more to let his city have the famous plane. His announced plan was to have a permanent hangar built for the aircraft at Memphis Municipal Airport, where it could be visited by the public.

The next thing was to select a crew - Morgan was contacted, but eventually proved unavailable. It was then announced that Captain Robert E. Little, the man originally picked by the committee, would do the piloting. Little had plenty of experience flying B-17s, although his war service had been in the Pacific, rather than Europe. He had flown 73 missions against Japan and was now a pilot for Chicago and Southern Airlines, making regular flights to Memphis.

On July 16, Captain Little and his crew boarded an Army Douglas C-47 transport belonging to the 4th Ferrying Group at Memphis, piloted by Captain Joseph P. Vecharelli and Major Millard A Webb and flew out to Altus. They didn't need a full crew of ten since nobody was needed to man the guns. The guns had been removed anyway. The crew of seven men who made the trip, other than Little, were all Air Force Reservists. They were Captain Robert. L. Taylor, navigator; Sergeant Percy Roberts, Jr., flight engineer; Technical Sergeant Charles Crowe, flight engineer; Lieutenant James Gowdy, second navigator; Captain Hamp Morrison, co-pilot,

The crew of the *Memphis Belle* seen at Altus before what was supposed to be her last flight. Bob Gray from the *Commercial Appeal* is seen kneeling, right. The '84' on the nose is the RFC catalog number. *[via Harry Friedman]*

Left: Bob Little and the returning crew, pose for photographs with staff from the RFC facility at Altus, and members of the Memphis Belle Girl Scout Troop also from Altus. [via Harry Friedman]

and Stuart Griffin, radio operator. Upon arrival they crawled all over the *Memphis Belle* , checking the aircraft over completely.

They were met by Burl Brumley, president of the Altus Chamber of Commerce, John Badger Chairman of the Chamber's Aviation Committee and Blackwood Saunders, Superintendent of the War Assets Administration. Later that day the met with Altus Mayor Fred Mains who presented them with a letter to deliver to Mayor Chandler: *'It is with a sad heart that we commit the Memphis Belle to your care. Expert mechanics have checked her daily and attendants have cleaned her regularly for a long time, for many thousands have come from all part of the country to see this famous ship. We took pride in having her at her best'.*

Bob Little: *The old gal gave us some trouble with the spark plugs, but Crowe and Roberts worked on the engines to make sure they got us to Memphis. The people at Altus asked if we wanted to make a test flight, but I told them no - when we get up there we are going all the way!'.* The next day they took off. There were still some problems, according to aviation editor Robert Gray of Memphis' morning newspaper, the *Commercial Appeal,* who was on the flight. The plane lifted off the runway but then the landing gear refused to retract. The crew had to use the emergency hand crank. Bob Little again: *'When we tried to raise the gear it wouldn't come up. So Percy [Roberts] got into the bomb bay and cranked it us as far as he could'.*

Percy Roberts, Jr: *'I was cranking the hell out of that thing and got the gear up about half way and it wouldn't go any more. So we came all the way to Memphis with the gear part down. On the way Little*

FERRY PERMIT, TEMPORARY REGISTRATION AND AIRWORTHINESS CERTIFICATE

Name __R. F. Little__

Address __Memphis, Tenn.__   Date __July 17, 1946__

This is your authority to ferry __Boeing__ aircraft, Model __B-17__

Army identification No. __41-24485__, Manufacturer's Serial Number

_____ date of manufacture _____. This temporary

certificate for ferry is valid only when the owner or his agent has

found this aircraft airworthy for the purpose of this flight and the

owner assumes all responsibility for such flight from __Altus, Oklahoma,__

to __Memphis, Tennessee.__

After the flight the attached Form ACA-501, properly executed, together
with DPC bill of sale should be presented to your local inspector for
assignment of registration number which must be painted on the aircraft
as set forth in Section 60.82 of the Civil Air Regulations. Application
(ACA-305) for an airworthiness certificate may be made to an Inspector
of the Administration. This certificate is valid only when flown by a
certificated pilot. No person other than a necessary and valid member
of the crew may be carried.

This authority expires upon arrival at the destination and not later

than __July 25, 1946__   (Date)

_____
Inspector, General Inspection Division

NOTE: ~~Title is subject aircraft transferred by DPC bill of sale or
quitclaim title below name is dated~~ _____

_____   __July 17, 1946__
D.P.C. Supervisor   Date

DISTRIBUTION:

Original, 1st copy: To Pilot; this copy must be presented by owner to
    Inspector at time of issuance of airworthiness certificate.

Duplicate, 2d copy: Forwarded by DPC to issuing Inspector to be forwarded
    to Inspector concerned.

Duplicate, 3d copy: Forwarded by DPC to issuing Inspector for filing with
    aircraft folder papers submitted to Washington.   (OVER)

The Ferry Permit issued to Bob Little for the flight from Altus to Memphis - this was to be the
Memphis Belle's last flight.

asked me if I wanted to fly it for a while. I told him sure, and it was not long before we had climbed a few hundred feet. He told me to look out at the left wing - then to look at the other. I was in a pretty good turn and did not even know it! Wasn't the prettiest thing, but I flew the Memphis Belle for about fifteen minutes'.

Then there was the matter of an in-flight fire. Percy Roberts again: 'Just west of Texarkana we smelt something burning and could not find it. We looked all over the aircraft until we discovered that someone had placed an oily rag over one of the electrical inverters. They get pretty hot in flight and the rag had started smouldering, sending some smoke up'.

Over Little Rock, Arkansas, the radio refused to work correctly - they could receive but not transmit. When they arrived over Memphis, Bob Little overflew the Tower and waggled his wings - a procedure to announce that their radio was out. Percy Roberts went back to the bomb bay and started to crank down the gear - but there was another problem - the down and locked indicators would not light up. 'She could have settled on to her belly as we put the tires on the runway. There was a bunch of fire trucks all over the place. I guess they thought we were going to have some real trouble when we landed' Roberts climbed into the ball turret to see if he could visually confirm they were 'down and locked'. As Gray later put it, Little '...greased her in' for a perfect landing and the Memphis Belle was home at last.

The crew that brought the *Memphis Belle* home! Left to right: Stuart Griffin, James Gowdy, Hamp Morrison, Bob Little, Mayor Walter Chandler, Percy Roberts, Bob Taylor and Charles Crowe. *[via Harry Friedman]*

The aircraft langished at the airport and in parking lots, slowly deteriorating. There was talk that it would move to the Smithsonian Institution in Washington DC, but nothing came of it. The crew moved on and away to other things. Margaret Polk briefly married but still lived in Memphis. Bob Morgan, meanwhile, moved on to other things and re-married - and re-married; eventually collecting six wives.

Meanwhile, the aircraft came under threat from Colonel Donald Fargo, commander of the 21st Air Division out at the airport who wanted to cut off the nose and use that as a memento in the Memphis Museum, while the remaining parts were used as training aids for Air Force Reserve personnel. In order to safeguard the aircraft, the Memphis American Legion, Post No. 1, agreed to adopt the *Memphis Belle* as a Legion project, placing the *Belle* on a conrete plinth in the grounds of the National Guard Armory, facing Central Avenue. There it was to remain from 1951 to 1977, when it came under the care and protection of the Memphis Belle Memorial Association, a group effectively founded by Memphian Frank Donofrio.

The aircraft was lifted off the plinth, dismantled and moved back out to the airport. Margaret Polk remembers the move from the Armory plinth: *'There was this little old guy who worked for Memphis Light, Gas and Water. He had wanted to start something and I was trying to help him. I remember the night before they moved the plane from the Armory, I sat in this little old boy's pick-up truck, talking to this little old boy who was guarding the plane until about 10 or 11 o'clock'.*

By 1980 basic restoration restoration work had started, and the *Memphis Belle* was parked near the Memphis Area Vocational Technical School, near the Airport, students at the school worked on the plane for months on end under the direction of their instructor Henry Martin. Here the first serious attempts at corrosion control, sheet metal repair and other work was undertaken, including some engine work and the complete restoration of the pilots and co-pilots instrument panel.

In the mid-1980s, following a long restoration process, the Tennessee Air National Guard became involved again, along with help from the 97th Bomb Wing at Blytheville Air Force Base, and another serious restoration program and re-painting began before installing the aircraft on Mud Island on the banks of the Mississippi. At one time there was a plan to use one of the Air Forces giant helicopters to move the aircraft the ten miles from the airport to Mud Island but there had been questions of the safety of such a lift. In the end it was decided that it would be done by a truck once more, as it had been done on the trips to and from the pedestal on Central, with her wings carefully removed.

The weekend of May 16/17 1987 would be THE weekend - it was an obvious choice, it was the anniversary of the day in 1943 when Robert K. Morgan and five members of his crew had completed their designated quota of 25 combat missions. A major part of the weekends celebrations would be a fly-over on each day by a number of B-17s arranged by Dr Harry Friedman. He contacted the owners of the eight flyable B-17s - seven said they could make it. The seven Flying Fortresses were organised under the auspices of the B-17 Co-Op - a group of owners, current pilots and restorers of the B-17 Flying Fortress and would be based at the West Memphis Airport, across the Mississippi River, where they would take part in a spectacular display open to the public during the weekend. The flyover was spectacular!

The *Memphis Belle* remained on Mud Island until late 2002 when the MBMA were forced to move again. But it was not just 'on display' - the MBMA already had laid in place an ongoing program of scheduled maintenance, corrosion control, continued acquisition of missing parts and equipment - much of which had been removed by the Air Force back in the late 1940s - at the same time as running a whole range of fund-raising and educational efforts. But they were fighting a losing battle against the elements and the very structure it was enclosed within. For a number of years the MBMA were searching around for a new home - they discovered it at the nearby US Navy airfield of Millington, to the north of the city.

The new home placed the aircraft in what could only be called a state-of-the art facility that included a climate-controlled environment and provided not only a restoration area but also storage and display facilities. It was not only an ideal home for the aircraft, but also for the restoration machinery donated by local and national aviation equipment manufacturers. Here a team of forty FAA-qualified aircraft mechanics from Fed Ex volunteered to overhaul the aircraft completely.

The aircraft was to remain at Millington for not quite two years. 41-24485 became a political football again, with machinations happening behind the scenes, and a whispering campaign being undertaken by some - targeting the MBMA - saying that not enough was being done to care for the aircraft and that it should be taken away from them. This coincided with a change of policy at the Air Force Museum whereby they and the Air Force would bring all 'significant' aircraft in their control worldwide together under one roof at Dayton.

Early in 2004 the US Air Force and the Air Force Museum sent yet another inspection team, which included Charles Metcalf and Richard Anderegg, the official Air Force historian. The inspection teams were accompanied by Bob Morgan. This was just one of several visits and meetings between the Air Force, the Air Force Museum and the MBMA during this period. - Indeed the Air Force came under pressure from certain congressmen and senators to give the MBMA more time and to provide them with both a format and timeframe prescribed by the Air Force Museum which would allow the aircraft to stay in Memphis. Once this had been agreed, research by the MBMA produced the realisation that the majority of citizens of the city Memphis were simply not interested in the *Memphis Belle*. Thus the MBMA requested the Air Force come get their aircraft.

Despite the fact that the aircraft has moved to Dayton, Ohio, The Memphis Belle Memorial Association continues to exist. In 2011 it arranged for a memorial to be erected in the Veterans Plaza, Overton Park, Memphis as a lasting monument to every crewmember who flew on the *Memphis Belle,* to Margaret Polk and to mark the aircraft's fifty-nine years in the city.

It is hoped that they continue with their task of educating future generations about the achievements of the aircraft and its crew.